Paula Modersohn-Becker

Brigitte Uhde-Stahl

Paula Modersohn-Becker

Belser Verlag
STUTTGART
ZURICH

Jacket illustration:
Paula Modersohn-Becker, SELF-PORTRAIT WITH HAND ON CHIN
c. 1906/07. Wood. 29 x 19,5 cm
Hanover, Niedersächsische Landesgalerie
(privately owned)

Address: Chr. Belser Verlag, Falkertstr. 73, D-7000 Stuttgart 1

English translation: Babel Translations, London
Reproductions: Grafisches Atelier Gerd Preiss, Gerlingen
Printed and bound in Germany 1990
ISBN 3-7630-0781-4

Distributed by Phaidon Press Limited, Oxford

Contents

The Woman, the artist and the person

When Paula Modersohn-Becker died suddenly at the age of thirty-one on 20 November 1907, hardly any of her contemporaries guessed that she would one day be reckoned among the avant-garde of modern art. Working quietly, all but concealed from the sight of her fellow-men, she had in the course of seven years created works that were to put her among the great "fathers" of modern art, on a par with Cézanne, van Gogh and Gauguin. Her works comprise over 600 studies and paintings and more than 1,000 drawings. In 1932, Rudolf Alexander Schröder recalled[1] the great astonishment with which he, Heinrich Vogeler and Otto Modersohn were seized as they looked through the works she left and gained a deeper insight into the wealth of her creativity:

"One day I found myself with Heinrich Vogeler in Modersohn's little studio in the schoolyard in Worpswede, where all the belongings of the deceased had been gathered. Most of what has now found its way into many houses and museums passed through our hands at that time. A wondrous day. We were filled with—and at the same time moved by—our sadness about the one who had been so abruptly torn from us, and by our ever-new astonishment at the positively inexhaustible wealth she left behind."

"We singled out and selected some individual works; we gathered the best items and classified them differently again if something even better came to light; [...]. But our amazement went far beyond what was present before us in the narrower sense. What shook us most of all was the traces left behind by a magnificent struggle, the intimation of a goal which may have been half concealed even to the soul of the struggler herself. Euphorion!"

Traces, intimations?

In view of her early death, her work was long regarded as fragmentary and incomplete. But Paula Modersohn-Becker's life was not accidentally "interrupted" at the age of thirty-one. It was "completed", observes Günter Busch, "and so too were her works, albeit that they consist in part of studies or sketches; but that probably applies to the artistic works which any visual artist has left for posterity. However, almost every record of her artist's hand—apart from her earliest artistic expressions produced as a learner—is, in a strange and rare manner, saturated with completeness. After no more than ten years of creativity, she left for posterity a true life-work consisting of well over 400 paintings and many times that number of freehand drawings. Anyone who can do this has a claim to be assessed not as an artistic beginner but as a master—even though each critical encounter with a particular work (...) brings forth her utterly unmistakable and very personal view of the world."[2]

The following remark by A.E. Brinckmann on the early death of many artists is reduced ad absurdum by Paula Modersohn-Becker's life, work and death: "This has caused an unimaginable loss to Western European intellectual culture."[3] This artist's life and work are witness to the maturing process, in the centre of which there stands the great departure captured by Rilke in the following verses:

O HERR, gieb jedem seinen eigenen Tod.
Das Sterben, das aus jenem Leben geht,
darin er Liebe hatte, Sinn und Not.
DENN wir sind nur die Schale und das Blatt,
Der große Tod, den jeder in sich hat.
das ist die Frucht, um die sich alles dreht.
("Grant us, o Lord, to each his final Rest,
A Dying which from his same Life may flow
Where Love, and Sense, and Need were manifest.
We are but Leaf and Husk, and naught besides;
But that same Death, which in each one resides,
—That is the Fruit about which all doth go.")

Not only did the importance to art history of Paula Modersohn-Becker's work go unrecognized, but it was also misunderstood for several decades. Thus Richard Hamann wrote in 1925 of "that auntie of Expressionism who paints everything roundly because she cannot manage any corners, and whose colours are so delicate because they are not really there at all, [...] who goes along with the revolutionary coarsenings of the new style, but goes only just far enough to make sure that the affectingly ugly features look even more affecting, [...] with whom it is always necessary to read aloud letters and diary pages when looking at her pictures, so that which has the outer appearance of pure art can utterly wallow in sentiment".[4] Or Carl Einstein[5] in 1926: "The sentimental, girlish non-art of the Worpswede group may have been accommodating towards female sensitivity. [...] Cézanne barely understood Modersohn. This talented, sensitive woman quietly became an 'Expressionist'; she timidly combined the austere kitsch of Nordic emotional singing with juicy Gauguin-like effects, and thus surprised us after her death in 1907. The best feature with Modersohn is her female sensitivity which utilizes, with loving gratitude, the not very valuable secondary material it receives."

Paula Modersohn-Becker's works are austere and reserved, and certainly not lovely, beautiful or even accommodating. But what induced these experts to err and make such unfounded remarks in their criticism? Arthur Fitger erred in similar fashion in 1899 when, in describing an exhibition, he criticized two paintings by this painter, who was still very young at the time. We shall return to this phenomenon later.

Her pictures were shown at only two exhibitions during her life. She sold only one picture to an outsider, and only a few to close friends. Initially, her own family—with the exception of her husband—was firmly convinced that nothing would become of her. She did not attract much attention until after her death. Memorial exhibitions held from 1908 onwards in Bremen, Hagen, Berlin, Hanover and Basle acquainted a broader section of the public with her work. Gustav Pauli, director of the Bremen Kunsthalle at that time, had always been in favour of Paula Modersohn-Becker's work and he published an early monograph in 1919.[6]

A collection of letters and diary entries appeared in 1917.[7] Rainer Maria Rilke had refused to edit this collection because he foresaw that, due to its incompleteness, it would falsify the impression it gave of the painter. It actually contributed to the creation of a kind of myth around Paula Modersohn-Becker, a myth closely associated with the romanticism of the Worpswede colony of artists. For many, she became the painter, rooted to the soil, of the Worpswede landscape, the painter of the homespun poor and old people of that region, the painter of children and motherhood plain and simple.

The Third Reich did her the honour of ostracizing her and confiscating some of her paintings as "degenerate".[8]

It was only after World War Two, and particularly in 1976 on the centenary of her birth, that scholars began to examine her work more closely. Several major jubilee exhibitions were held. Her complete surviving letters and diaries were finally published in 1979[9], so that good conditions now exist for a close study of Paula Modersohn-Becker's life and work.

An initial subject for regret is that Paula Modersohn-Becker's work had little effect and found no followers.[10] As many as 80 years had to pass before another generation of people was, perhaps, better able to understand how unique her work is in more than one way. From her paintings there speaks a spirituality towards which we of today seem more receptive. There are at least indications that the rational and materialist way of thinking which was previously dominant is being supplemented, and to some extent corrected, by a new understanding of reality, rather more feminine and intuitive in character. This feminine spirituality is strongly marked in Paula Modersohn-Becker. Her holistic way of existing, her ability to associate herself lovingly with people and things and to experience and accept herself as part of nature—these are features which we are now able to appreciate with a concern entirely different from anything possible during her life.

She was obviously far ahead of her time. The disintegration of the times in which she lived was felt by contemporaries to be something new and intense, but she did not react to it by "shouting", by reflecting the depths and abysses of her own soul as the Expressionists often did in their painting and poetry. Instead, she unrelentingly endeavoured to achieve a unity beyond her own subjectivity, and she found it on a higher suprapersonal level, on a level of being which lies beyond the surface of things. She felt this striving for unity to be a task that encompassed all of her. She wanted to be a human being, as a woman, as a mother, as an artist. She finally succeeded in this on all levels. This struggle, which she herself continuously felt to be difficult, can be seen in her works. This, quite apart from the high artistic quality of her pictures, is a further reason to make the acquaintance of this painter again.

"If you really have a talent..."

Dresden and Bremen, 1876–1896

Paula Becker was born on 8 February 1876, the third of seven children.

The German Reich under Wilhelm I and Bismarck was just five years old in 1876. The period of rapid industrial expansion had begun: a time of economic growth and relative political stability. Industrialization was proceeding apace and was bringing about fundamental changes in society and in ways of living in that society.

In the course of this development, women started to become more self-confident. They were endeavouring to find a place in a world dominated by men and to attain the same status as men in the fields of teaching, research and politics. The "Victorian age", in its last agonies, resisted the great transformations of that era in an attempt, doomed to failure, "to keep alive anaemic ideals while preserving middle-class respectability".[11]

As regards the severe problems brought about by industrialization—the German Socialist Workers' Party was founded in 1875—it was optimistically believed that they could be solved with the aid of science and technology. In those cases where social hardship in the cities was impossible either to eliminate or to overlook, people repressed it into their subconscious. The end of the 19th century was a period of psychological repression, something which could be arrived at by taking refuge in pleasure. Those addicted to pleasure used to congregate in centres such as Montmartre near Paris. Thus it was that the era acquired the name "belle époque".

But it was not only the social problems that were repressed. Another matter repressed was what the sensitive members of that generation felt, usually with some anxiety, to be new, nay, alien–a human dimension whose first systematic investigator was Dr. Sigmund Freud. From the viewpoint of the psychoanalysis he developed, and in its language, this matter was the "unconscious"—a realm of experience which, in another kind of perception (e.g. mystic perception), communicates itself as being the "depths of the soul" or (in Rilke) as "the interior of the world". This realm of experience, which at that time was a new discovery and a new formulation, first gained literary form in the image of the "depths of the sea" in Ibsen's "Wild Duck" of 1884. The first person to give it expression in visual art was Edvard Munch. "The great and promising feature of Munch's work", wrote Stanislaw Przybyzewski in 1894[12], "is that all those depths and darknesses for which language has not yet found any corresponding sounds [...] and which only express themselves as a dark foreboding compulsion are clothed in colour in Munch's works and enter the onlooker's consciousness."

Finally, the conventional view of the world was rocked to its foundations by physics when Einstein, in his relativity theory of 1905, did not merely "relativize" the then current ideas concerning space and time, but positively uprooted them.

This was a necessarily only fragmentary sketch of the background against which Paula Modersohn-Becker's work must be seen. For an artist's works are never produced in isolation from the political, material and intellectual circumstances of the times. The times form the fertile soil for the artist's creativity, and he gives back to that soil a transformed picture of the times.[13]

When Paula Modersohn-Becker was born, the family lived in Dresden-Friedrichstadt, where her father, Carl Woldemar Becker, was an engineer employed by the Berlin-Dresden Railway. Her mother, Mathilde von Bültzingslöwen, came from Lübeck. Both families originally came from Saxon Thuringia.

The Beckers had a close and warm family life, Paula's mother being the more enterprising, cheerful and vital partner. Paula's father tended to be depressed, warned the family that they should be sensible, and was a restraining and sceptical influence. Paula Becker had a close relationship with him and with her mother, and she was particularly hurt because her father never recognized her as an artist.

The children's mother took care that they were educated as befitted their social class. Specifically, the daughters were to learn all the skills required for middle-class education. These included piano-playing, foreign languages, a knowledge of literature and music and, last but not least, a good and assured command of the etiquette required by the numerous social events in which the family took part.

An important event occurred in Paula Becker's childhood, but it was only many years later that she told Rilke of its deep significance. This was her encounter with death. She was ten years old when she was buried in a sandpit when playing with ten other children. She herself was saved, but her cousin Cora Parizot, who was older than she, died. "This child was the first event in my life. [...] We met at the age of nine and loved each other very much. She was very mature and intelligent. It was with her that the first glimmerings of awareness entered my life."[14] Who can fathom how deeply such an event moulds a young person's character? Death crops up repeatedly in the evidence Paula Backer gives concerning herself; she seems to encounter it repeatedly, as being the opposite pole of a life experienced with great joy and intensity.

The family moved to Bremen in 1888, when she was twelve. There her father took up a similar position to that in Dresden with the Prussian Railway Management in the area of the State of Bremen. He was appointed Prussian Government Building Surveyor in 1890. The family moved into an official flat in the house at 29 Schwachhäuser Chaussee.

This move did not merely take the family into a new and unknown world; the family now found itself in a society which was moulded by Hanseatic mercantile and seafaring traditions and found it difficult to absorb any new elements. It was through the outgoing sincerity of Paula Becker's mother that the family was able nevertheless to fit itself, to a satisfactory degree, into the new society. The Beckers' house, despite its simplicity, became a place where people, mostly young, liked to meet informally for discussions, singing, theatrical performances and tennis. It was in this atmosphere of warmth and lively openness that Paula Becker spent her Bremen schooldays.[15]

Shortly after being confirmed in the spring of 1892, Paula Backer went to stay for a year with relatives in England, the aim being that she should learn English and housekeeping on a country estate near London. Her first letters, which, along with her diary, are the most important biographical source, stem from this period. Letters were the link that held the family together, even over long distances. Of course, neither the letters nor the diary entries were intended for outsiders—a fact that should always be borne in mind.

The regular and often humorous letters tell us of the tasks which Paula's severe aunt Marie Hill imposed on her. "I've just made twelve whole pounds of butter all by myself, and of course I'm terribly proud of it . . .," she wrote to her grandmother.[16]

We also read of her first experience with her own artistic creativity. The earliest mention is in a letter to her father[17]: "I had another sketching lesson today.[18] I am doing my first landscape in sepia only. It looks a little as if I had painted it during a downpour, but it's going to turn out well! I really wanted to include some living creatures; but when I had half-finished a goose, I laid her down (she herself lay down!) and after I had just drawn a horse's head, it was taken to the stable and of course I don't have enough imagination to think up the rest of the horse."

We do not know how Paula Becker began drawing and painting or when she decided to pursue her favourite occupation professionally. In any event her mother supported her in this intention, and her English uncle enabled her to take lessons at Mr. Ward's school of drawing in London from October 1892 onwards. She wrote enthusiastically of her lessons in her letters home. It was at that school that she began a traditional academic education of the kind which had been usual since the time of Leonardo and whose stages were strictly followed. It consisted of: drawing from simple, two-dimensional models; drawing from three-dimensional models (usually casts, reliefs or jointed dolls); drawing from nature, i.e. from living models.

After some initial shyness, she sent some samples of her work to Bremen, and her father took them seriously: "We got your first attempts in Indian ink and, instead of the scorn you were expecting, they've all met with recognition."[19] His commentaries and advice in the same letter display a knowledge of the matter: "If you now go to London, I hope you'll have the opportunity to see some drawings and paintings. Don't study their inner meaning, but study their form; it's the form that is the main thing in art, however little a disciple of art may realize it at the outset. The finest idea is no use if the performance doesn't accord with the inner meaning."

By saying this her father was opposing the superficial behaviour and the activities of dilettante artists who worked with very little knowledge and with whom he was comparing the work of serious artists. He had probably himself been trained as a draughtsman when preparing for his modern technical profession. Paula Becker evidently did not follow her father's suggestion to study the outer form of some drawings and paintings. She does not seem to have taken notice of the modern English artists who had been trained in French painting, neither did she apparently visit the London galleries with their avant-garde pictures on display.

In a later letter[20], Paula's father promised her to give her the opportunity for further artistic training in Germany: "If you really have a talent for drawing and painting, I'll certainly be delighted to try to have you given further training here

1
Paula Becker, c. 1895.

2
Self-Portrait
1893
Charcoal, 39.7 x 27.5 cm
Privately owned

in Germany, so that you'll be able to work independently later on. What with the abrupt transformation to which we are being subjected as regards earthly possessions in our present times, and what with the strenuous labour that the battle for existence brings with it, every girl must strive to become independent if need be."

If you really have a talent? Who is to decide that? What yardstick will be applied?

Her father, who ran the domestic economy of a large family, had a realistic idea of material living conditions. When making the above statement, what he may have had in mind was that Paula should train to be a drawing teacher, a much sought-after profession for women in those days.[21] But his conception of art was moulded by 19th-century art, and he therefore never really succeeded in grasping the dimensions of Paula's talent or her artistic development. This was why he was never fully able to acknowledge her as an artist, and this was a great source of concern to his daughter, who began to withdraw from him more and more.

Her stay in England ended prematurely. It was the first time Paula Becker had been away from home and, being sixteen, she was still very young. She began to be homesick, and her physical condition finally deteriorated so much that she was allowed to go home to Bremen in Christmas 1892.

It was only some months later that she was able to bring herself to tell her aunt in a letter[22] of what had become so intolerable to her during her stay in England. This letter shows the astonishing insight this seventeen-year-old had into the darker side of her nature and that she also came to grips with that darker side. Towards her aunt—and then again and again throughout her life—she had to cope with being blamed for her "egoism".

Viewed externally, the England project ended in renunciation and escape. But this period meant a great deal to Paula's inner development: her first intensive concern with her own artistic activities, a painful friction with new, unwontedly strict surroundings, and—in her painful contact with those surroundings—contact with herself as a first stage towards self-recognition and maturity. One significant fact is that Paula retained particular confidence in her aunt Marie Hill, so that the best information about her inner development is to be found in her letters to her aunt.

Initially, Paula was once again a child in her own family. Her father fulfilled his promise and had Bernard Wiegandt the painter give her drawing lessons. Besides helping about the house, she once again enjoyed untroubled youth to the full: she danced, skated and pursued social activities before beginning, at her father's insistence, a two-year training course at the Bremen training college for women teachers. During this period she hardly had a chance to continue her artistic endeavours.

In 1895, the year in which she completed her training at the age of nineteen, her father was prematurely retired because the Bremen Railway Traffic Department closed down. Despite making great efforts, he could not find a new post and became increasingly negative and depressed in the period that followed.

"I now experience everything with my eyes..."

Berlin, 1896–1898

Paula Becker travelled to Berlin in April 1896 to attend a six-week course at the drawing and painting school of the "1867 Association of Berlin Women Artists". The six weeks became two years. She lived with relatives in Schlachtensee. Her mother took in women boarders so as to pay for the painting classes.

In those days women found it hard to gain training in drawing and painting. Art had always been regarded as a male domain in middle-class circles. For women, art was only a social grace which should, if possible, not go beyond dilettantism. If a woman worked for herself and was socially independent, this smacked of subversion and danger and was regarded as unfeminine. But woman's emancipation in the field of art could not be stopped in the long term. In France, women artists joined to form the "Union des Femmes Artistes" with its own annual "Salon des Femmes". It was not until 1897 that they were admitted to study at the Paris Ecole des Beaux-Arts, the leading academy of art in France.[23]

At the turn of the century, the art academies of the German Reich were not yet open to women, so that Paula Becker had to seek her training in a drawing and painting school founded by female initiative. The school she selected had a good reputation.

Berlin itself was in the process of becoming the cultural as well as the political capital of the German Reich.[24] It was true that a conservative academism still dominated at the Prussian Academy of Arts. But efforts to enhance the standing of modern trends in art were everywhere making themselves felt. In 1892, certain artists, including Walter Leistikow and Max Liebermann, joined to form the "Group of the Eleven", from which the Berlin Secession proceeded in 1898. Art dealers, in particular, were given an international function as agents who, operating independently of any institution, brought the most modern paintings into their galleries. Museums—especially the Nationalgalerie under Hugo von Tschudi—, art writers such as Julius Meier-Graefe, private sponsors, and highbrow art journals such as "Pan" and the Munich magazine "Jugend", all contributed to introducing a broader public to the works of Impressionism and Neoimpressionism.

Having arrived in Berlin, the twenty-year-old Paula Becker now energetically took charge of herself and her artistic development. This was the Paula of whom her father wrote to her mother that she was "pretentious and does little work, very little. [...] Even at home she is only a sullen soul..."[25]. But she

3
Berlin, c. 1897, Paula Becker on right.

recognized her own law and followed it. Thus she wrote to her aunt Marie Hill in England[26]: "I must conduct a secret quarrel with the world outside, otherwise I shall be unfit for the world, [...], I have made up my mind to use my horns and feelers not to knock against others with, but to push myself quietly along my path in life."

Following this law, she threw herself into her work with tremendous intensity, seeming to look up from it only occasionally to give an account of it to her parents, as here:

"I work with a passion which excludes everything else. I often feel like a hollow cylinder with a steam piston moving up and down at breakneck speed inside it."[27] In her "dry times", she always paused for breath. This intensity was to continue until the end of her life.

While she was now doing exactly what no one could take away from her, namely continuing her artistic training, those around her contributed to the material support of this work. In late 1897, when her father insistently impressed upon her that she should at last take up a position as governess, she received an inheritance from some relatives, and also a certain monthly sum for three years so that she could continue studying in peace.

At school in Berlin, she followed the tradition of artistic training by first drawing heads, and then nudes from life. Her media were firstly charcoal, and then also red chalk, pastels and water-colours. Towards the end of the year, she discovered oil paints for herself and was enthusiastic about them. She finally joined Jeanne Bauck's portrait-painting class and felt very well there. She set great store by the thorough work which the teacher required, and also by the "great simple conception"[28] in each of her pictures.

Apart from the work she did at school, and also of her own accord at home, she was untiring in her visits to exhibitions and museums. She soaked it all up like a dry sponge. In Berlin, as well as on some trips elsewhere[29], she came to grips with the works of Dürer, Rembrandt, Michelangelo, Botticelli and others. It was here that she made the acquaintance of the contemporary paintings by Edvard Munch and the French artists. Thus the desire to go to Paris herself one day may have arisen within her while she was in Berlin.

These years were also a time of reading and visits to the theatre. The works of Gerhart Hauptmann and Henrik Ibsen particularly stimulated her in her restless seeking.

4
Standing Male Nude
1896/97
Charcoal, 62 x 42 cm
Privately owned

Finally, a letter and a diary entry from the first few weeks of her stay in Berlin are both very informative as regards her artistic development.

On 23 April 1896 she wrote to her parents (BT 79 f.): "As I walk along, I have immense pleasure in studying physiognomies and I try quickly to discover their characteristic features. When I am talking to someone, I diligently observe the shadow cast by the nose, and I see how the deep shadow on the cheek commences energetically, only to blend with the light again. I think that this blending is the most difficult part. I am still giving too much force to every shadow I draw. I am still putting too many irrelevant things down on paper instead of bringing out what is important. For it is only then that life and blood come into the matter. My heads are still too wooden and immobile. [...] Rembrandt really knows how to manage the shadows, and that is why I am so interested in him."

About three weeks later, she then wrote down in her diary[30]: "I am still having immense difficulty with the material. I find it awfully difficult to use the charcoal in this dashing way. [...] Tremendously difficult! Always keeping an eye on the whole picture, when at present I can always only see the individual object. I now experience everything with my eyes, and look at everything from the painter's point of view. When I am wandering along the Potsdamerstrasse on my way to drawing school, I observe a thousand faces that go past me, and I try to discover their essential features at a glance. It's very amusing [...]. Then I try to see everything in two dimensions and to resolve the rounded lines into angled ones. But it is tremendous fun." And further down: "I still look at many things in a childish and unpractised way, in too small-minded a way and so on."

These sentences, flung down almost unconsciously, indicate that the germ of what would one day make her paintings great already slumbered within her, and that her development was proceeding extraordinarily rapidly.

From the very first day of her stay in Berlin, she practised not only painting and drawing, but also that process of perception which is essential to the work of an artist: vision. The observation of a shadow in a face, as she describes it in April, is still based on the object conceived as a three-dimensional body. Willi Baumeister describes such vision as "körperhaftes" ("corporeal") or "nutzbringendes" ("productive") vision.[31] In this form of vision, the person seeing uses an idea gained from experience to take brightness, darkness and coloured forms and to re-shape them into the surfaces of physical things and of the spatial relationships associated with those things. Contrasting with this there is another form of vision, which Paula Becker described in her diary in May and which Willi Baumeister refers to as "Schauen" ("looking"). This lies beyond rational registration and records all the phenomena perceived by the eye, taking them to be purely visual phenomena. This means that looking is "the most important point of departure for all artistic painting, because it is also the most all-embracing."[32]

As can be seen from the second quotation, Paula Becker practises this pure two-dimensional "looking". Both quotations prove that such looking is not a passive but a very active process. In addition, the second quotation makes it clear that the artistic process begins with the seeing process, where what is looked at is transformed by purely artistic categories into painted and angular features. But the process of seeing and transformation described here is a precondition for the creation of a new, non-illusionist type of painting. Thus, without being directly influenced, and evidently working entirely of her own accord, Paula Becker prepared herself for an encounter with the works of Cézanne, which she was to experience as if they were a "thunderstorm".

The second factor, which she referred to in both letter and diary entry, and also again and again later on, refers more to the level of the statement being made in her paintings. But that level—at least in her works—is never detached from formal matters. Even in pure "looking", she attempts to distinguish essential from inessential matters and then to put down on paper only what is "important", so that the matter is filled with "life and blood".

These sentences are the first time that Paula Becker, still expressing herself in a dreamlike and unconscious way, put her artistic goal into words: by doing without the manifold visible details, and by a formal reduction to what is "essential", she aimed to come closer to the life of things, which lies beyond their optical appearance. She characteristically practised by observing people, and portraits were to become her favourite pictorial subject.

These exercises were bound to have an effect on her personal development. Conrad Fiedler wrote in 1887: "a whole new path for the development of his [the artist's] awareness of reality opens up before him" when he practises "seeing for its own sake".[33] In that essay he gave a detailed investigation of the origins of artistic activity, and the results he arrived at are still valid today. A concentrated and purely visual perception, detached from ego-based feeling and thinking, expands the total ability to perceive and also assists in a more objective perception of oneself. This comes close to certain forms of meditative practices. Thus, distinguishing essential from inessential matters may have been an important preparation for what Paula Becker strove after all her life, both in herself and in her works: to be plain and simple.

Several passages in the letters she wrote at the beginning of her time in Worpswede show that Paula Becker was also able to revel perfectly "normally" in the beauty of landscape and nature, acting emotionally and romantically like other girls and women of her time of life and her era.

The pictures from the Berlin period show the young painter's great artistic curiosity and range. She practised various stylistic tendencies, ranging from rapid, Impressionistic-looking sketches in oils to sheets unmistakably reflecting the interest she took in Jugendstil works. The two-dimensional mode of depiction adopted by the Jugendstil, with its emphasized lines, fitted in with her own endeavours, whereas the somewhat decorative element, with the emphasis on the foreground, to be found in Jugendstil works was essentially alien to her goals. In any event, she continued, right into the first years of her Worpswede period, during which she was mainly influenced by Heinrich Vogeler, to produce some etchings and commercial designs associated with the Jugendstil.

A considerable number of drawings which she produced independently of her school activities have survived from her Berlin period. Drawing was part of the basic artistic training at academies, and Paula Becker practised finger exercises of this kind all her life. In addition, she recorded impressions in sketches, and tried many experiments in draughtsmanship when working on a particular subject which she then elaborated in a painting. Her water-colours and gouaches, spontaneously and rapidly cast down on to the paper, were never regarded by her as independent pictures which might be published one day, but as pictorial ideas upon which she worked creatively. Thus it is that the quality of her drawings is very variable. From the beginning of her artistic activities onwards she produced dilettante and unsuccessful charcoal and pencil drawings which were drily academic, naturalistic or expressively temperamental, but she also produced drawings that look like complete pictures. In her later years her drawings became increasingly economical. With a few pertinent strokes she achieved the compression and simplicity she had always been striving after in this artistic medium too.

One study from the Berlin period that does make a valid pictorial statement is the pastel PORTRAIT OF LADY WITH HAT AND VEIL from 1897 (Ill. I).

The head shown in three-quarter profile is moulded in three dimensions by using soft shadows and gentle highlights. The horizontal of the hat, the vertical and diagonal of the outlined veil, and the broadly spread black of the shoulders, all go to fix the portrait firmly on the surface of the picture. The portrait has been moved away from the middle of the picture in such a way that the edge of the picture cuts through the lady's left shoulder. This gives the picture a certain inner dynamism.

The colours are limited to a harmony of black and brownish-beige. By taking a closer look at the original, the onlooker can—even in this early pastel—gain an insight into the tremendous range of differentiation in the use of colour. Other colours are woven into the main colours in a manner that is barely noticeable but determines the picture's lively effect. A breath of green lies upon the summarily treated black of the dress. The artist passed an orange chalk over the left nostril and above the left eye. A dab of blue below the left ear suggests an earring and introduces a new accent to the two-colour harmony.

The SELF-PORTRAIT from this period (c. 1898; Ill. II) also uses the artistic language which was widespread in Europe at that time and united a moderately realistic mode of depiction with the bright colours and dissolved surface structure of Impressionism. Paula Becker does not yet put into effect in her picture the knowledge gained from purely looking at things. But a feature characteristic of her personal style is that closeness to the onlooker which results from the strong impression this picture makes of having been cut out of something. The intensity of her gaze is not merely to be explained by the fact that she was painting in front of a mirror.

With some 30 self-portraits that were painted and 20 that were drawn, Paula Becker joins such painters as Dürer, Rembrandt, van Gogh, Corinth and Beckmann who frequently depicted themselves.[34]

The first drawing to have survived was produced by the sixteen-year-old Paula in 1893. She explained the advantage of drawing or painting self-portraits in a letter to her brother Kurt: "One thing about me is that I do not exactly idealize people, rather the reverse. I gave Mr. Bischoff such a furious State official's face that he departed from us thinking thoughts of vengeance. Since then I have been drawing my own dear image in the mirror, but that is at least tolerant."[35] In addition, Paula could use herself as a model who was available free of charge at all times. To her, the act of coming artistically to grips with her own visible form meant in the final analysis that she was conducting a serious dialogue with herself. Every self-portrait was a milestone along the road of her self-questioning and self-knowledge; indeed, the question "Who am I?" lies behind every self-portrait. It is characteristic that she never painted herself as an impressive painter, but always as a private person on the road to self-knowledge. This was a path she pursued with such consistency that she was in later years able to portray herself in the nude.

In summer 1898, Paula Becker concluded her years of apprenticeship in Berlin by going on a trip to Norway to which her generous uncle Wulf von Bültzingslöwen had treated her.

"Here in this solitude..."

Worpswede, 1898–1899

In September 1898, after her of apprenticeship years, in Berlin, Paula Becker, now aged twenty-two, moved to Worpswede near Bremen. This poor village, still famous today for the Worpswede artists' colony, lies on the edge of a large area of moorland some fifteen miles north-east of Bremen. Beginning in 1884, painters such as Fritz Mackensen, Otto Modersohn, Hans am Ende, Fritz Overbeck, Heinrich Vogeler and finally Carl Vinnen had retreated to it.[36]

Their great models were the painters of the Dachau colony and of the "school of Barbizon" near Fontainebleau, who flourished around the mid-19th century and whose best-known representative was Jean François Millet (1814–1875). Like those painters, the Worpswede group wished to stand outdoors before their subject and paint landscapes that were not idealized, but natural and atmospheric. They also took their motifs from peasant life.

Paula Becker had seen pictures by this group of painters in the Bremen Kunsthalle in 1895, and she told her brother Kurt about them[37]: "They have now put on an exhibition, and some of the exhibits are really fabulous." Paula, who was nineteen at the time, had her own way of commenting on individual painters and paintings. On Mackensen's "Sermon on the Heath" of 1895, she wrote: "How true to life the artist has been in portraying the individual life-sized figures. They're all full of life. Of course, they're all very realistically done, but it's quite fabulous work."

The word "but" betrays what she thinks, or will later think, of a realistic mode of depiction. She does not understand the perspective in Mackensen's picture, and she asks herself the following question, rich in consequences: "Is that right, and is our foreshortened perspective only something artificially inculcated into us?" For the moment she has a negative answer to this question: "I cannot think that that is so." But a year later–let us remember her letter and diary entry from the Berlin period–she will be consciously practising the "non-perspective"[38] way of looking.

She was also "tremendously" interested "in a certain Modersohn. He has portrayed the various moods of the heathland so beautifully. His water is so transparent and his colours so singular".

But Heinrich Vogeler is given a bad mark: "... he has done some crazy things. He paints the whole of nature in a stylized way, as was done in the Pre-Raphaelite period. In the present century one can only shake one's head at such jests." But two years later, positively enraptured, she wrote of him in her diary[39]: "a lucky fellow", "my real darling. He is not such a realist as Mackensen. He lives in a world of his own." His paintings, shaped by the Jugendstil (Paula's pictures are often slightly reminiscent of them), "have a moving effect on me. He used the old German masters as his model. His forms are very severe, stiffly severe. [...] This is Vogeler, that little fellow. Isn't he charming?" She later came to a very good understanding with Vogeler. But he took no notice of her as an artist during her lifetime, then after her death he tried to make up for this by becoming very involved with her art.

In summer 1897—Paula Becker was still living in Berlin at that time—she felt the desire, while on a family outing to Worpswede, to spend some weeks there painting during the summer holidays. Thus it was that she came to love this country and its colours, in the summer of 1897. She visited various painters at that time. She saw Otto Modersohn only once in this period, and of him she wrote in her diary[40]: "All I can remember is a tall thing in a brown suit with a reddish beard." There was something soft and sympathetic in his eyes, she wrote. The description of Modersohn ends with the words: "I should like to get to know this Modersohn."

The land that Paula Becker entered upon and painted in autumn of 1898 was described by the poet Rilke as follows: "It is a strange country. Standing on the small sandy mountain of Worpswede, one can see it spread out all around, like those peasants' cloths which show the corners of deeply glimmering flowers on a dark background. It lies there flat, almost without a crease, and the paths and watercourses lead far into the horizon, where a sky of indescribable changeability and greatness begins. This sky is reflected in every leaf. Everything seems to be concerned with the sky; it is everywhere. And the sea is everywhere. The sea which no longer exists, which once rose and fell here thousands of years ago and whose sand dune was the sandy mountain on which Worpswede stands. The things cannot forget the sea. The great rushing sound that fills the old pine trees on the mountain seems to be the sea's rushing, and the wind, the wide and mighty wind, brings with it the scent of the sea. The sea is the history of the land. The land hardly has any other past."[41]

Paula Becker became completely immersed in this natural world. She allowed herself to be borne along by it in her moods and feelings. She experienced nature as something animated. In the rhythm of growing and passing away she felt the strength of something living, of which she knew she was a part. Her relationship with nature was essentially deeply religious; in nature she found something of God, although she scarcely dared pronounce His name.

Paula Becker did not have any ties with the Christianity of the Church. In this, her way of thinking was very similar to that of the open-minded middle-class citizens of her time, for whom Christianity no longer played a leading rôle and who were rather fulfilling a middle-class obligation by being members of a church. Paula Becker's education at school and in confirmation classes had given her a good knowledge of the Bible, which did not though block her path to an immediate experience of God, in nature for example. "I say God and by that I mean the spirit which pervades nature, the spirit of which I too form a tiny part and which I can feel in a great storm."[42]

Nature brought her closer and closer to herself. "Here in this solitude, man reduces himself to himself alone", she wrote in her diary in early 1899.[43] "It is a strange feeling to know that all the variegated, inculcated play-acting which I used to possess is falling away and being replaced by a vibrating simplicity. I am working on myself. I am reworking myself, part knowingly, part unconsciously. I am changing; is it for the good? Whatever the case, I am becoming

I
Portrait of Lady With Hat and Veil
c. 1897
Pastel, 48.6 x 62.3 cm
Bremen, Kunsthalle

II
Self-Portrait
c. 1898
Oil on cardboard, 28.2 x 23 cm
Bremen, Kunsthalle

III
Self-Portrait
With Parisian Houses in Background
1900
Paper on canvas, 38 x 35.5 cm
Bremen, privately owned

IV
Sandpit on the Weyerberg
Dated at lower left: 1899
Cardboard, 55 x 74 cm
Munich, Bavarian State Collections

V
Birchtrees in Autumn
1900
Oil distemper on cardboard, 47 x 28 cm
Fischerhude, Otto-Modersohn-Museum

VI
Worpswede Landscape
Dated at lower left: 1900
Oil on cardboard, 53 x 40.4 cm
Hanover, State Museum of Lower Saxony

VII
Ditch on the Moor
c. 1900/1902
Oil distemper on canvas, 54.1 x 33 cm
Privately owned

VIII
PERAMBULATOR WITH GOAT AND CHILDREN
1905
Oil on cardboard, 33.9 x 49.6 cm
Wuppertal, Von der Heydt Museum

more progressive, purposeful and independent." In April 1900, Heinrich Vogeler reacted to her efforts, stating: "Incidentally, you have changed enormously to your own advantage in your last few years here; you have become so free of conventional poetical requirements. In fact, I would not previously have been able to write you such a crazy letter based on the simple mood that is moving me just now."[44]

It makes a great impression to follow Paula Becker pursuing a path similar to that which may also be observed in Jawlensky: the path of inner development, which C.G. Jung, in the language of depth psychology, describes as the individuation process. But while Jawlensky finds his way towards wholeness by means of meditation and the Christian religion—and of course also by artistic work—, the means by which Paula Becker makes contact with existence and her higher self lies—apart from in her work as an artist—also in the nature around her.

The other great subject matter of her early Worpswede period consists of portraits of people from the surrounding area. Here, Paula Becker preferred to take her models from the poor-house, not merely because they were "cheaper", but because, with her loving gaze, she saw the simple, untheatrical and unadorned aspect of these people. She was never interested in pillorying political or social conditions, something which Käthe Kollwitz regarded it as her task to do in Berlin. Paula Becker had no "talent" for politics, without interest in day-to-day politics, and was in some respects even conservative in her affection for things German. This also applied to her attitude towards questions of women's emancipation, which was in full swing in her day. She lived and worked on other spiritual and intellectual planes. But her effect was no less for that. Or is this the very reason why she is still relevant today?

For her, peasants, poor people and children were all part of Mother Nature. Sensitive as she was, she never attempted to be so ingratiating as to overcome the detachment that separated her from them. But it may certainly be regarded as a peculiar—human—achievement of hers that she managed to induce these people to sit for her, even in the nude. Rainer Maria Rilke described these people as follows: "Something of the sadness and homelessness of their fathers is still on them [...]; the smiling of the mothers is not passed on to the sons, because the mothers never did smile. They all have only one face: the hard, tense face of work [...]. The hearts of these bodies are oppressed and cannot develop. Their minds are freer and have been through a certain one-sided development. Not a deepening, but a sharpening towards resourcefulness, gibing and wittiness."[45]

Paula and Fritz Mackensen reached an agreement to the effect that he would, at regular intervals, look at Paula's paintings and suggest improvements. This became a strict and systematic course of instruction[46], in which Clara Westhoff and Ottilie Reyländer also took part. In June 1899, Marie Bock is mentioned as being the fourth pupil. Under Mackensen's guidance, many drawn portraits of peasants were produced. They are closely related to the portraits by Paula's fellow-pupils, and reflect Mackensen's goal of "conceiving of 'simple man' as someone heroic and conferring upon him a general dignity going beyond the immediate occasion" (see PEASANT WOMAN SPINNING, c. 1899, Ill. 5).

To begin with, Paula Becker was very satisfied with this course of instruction, but she soon observed that they would come to a parting of the ways. Her conception, which differed from Mackensen's, manifested itself in a number of

5
Peasant Woman Spinning
c. 1899
Charcoal, 80 x 54 cm
Frankfurt, privately owned

6
Girl Seated
c. 1899/1900
Charcoal on paper, 121.5 x 52.8 cm
Bremen, Ludwig-Roselius collection

large-sized drawings of nudes (see Girl Seated, c. 1899/1900, Ill. 6).

In these, the physical imperfections of the models are "depicted with a positively piercing fascination". The considerations which lay behind this tendency may be found in a letter of June 1899 to her brother Kurt[47], in which she tells him of the effect produced by reading works by Ibsen: "I believe that I am learning a lot by reading. I am learning a particular way of observing people, and this will then have an effect on my art. I have quite a good knowledge of people but, probably due to Mother's influence, there is an idealized streak about it. But the close relationship I now have with nature has made me take the view that naturalism is the only proper course to take. This is because naturalism requires a far greater diversity of different individuals, something which is impossible in idealism. Idealism generalizes. I also used to generalize. And in my view the greatest progress I have made this winter lies in the fact that I no longer generalize or at least intend no longer to generalize. Greater clarity has come into my being. That makes me glad."

Thus the reduction found in her later pictures is based on a precise observation and an unbeautified way of depicting human beings.

The unusually large size of these nude drawings, the reproduction of the model either strictly frontally or in profile, the use of black or other colours to cover the whole surface of the picture, and indeed the entire intensity of the conception: all this gives the nude drawings a painting-like, almost monumental effect.

Mackensen thought that the way Paula Becker deviated from his own idea showed a beginner's incompetence: "Apart from the fact that until then I had only given Heinrich Vogeler some suggestions, this lady [Paula Becker] was, in contrast to him, a complete beginner and, in the ladies' art school from which she came, had lost her way towards even beginning to be a painter. Here she started assiduously painting away although she had no feeling for organic matters and no control of form—two matters which are the necessary firm foundation for the acquisition of painting skills. So I was obliged to disappoint her greatly straight away. But she soon saw the need for change and, with an energy that astonished me, she plunged into the work of studying heads and nudes."[48]

Probably acting on her teacher's advice, Paula Becker often used to draw in her sketch books at this time. The pages are full of practice drawings and aides-mémoires for later work. She seems in these sketches to have found the style of her future pictures. In some of the drawings (see Ill. 7) of those early years, the style can be identified as her unmistakable independent handwriting.

In the charcoal drawing Dreeben Seated Facing Right dating from 1899 (Ill. 8), the old woman from the poor-house, who repeatedly appears, even in the artist's last and most mature works, is seen in severe profile. Anecdotal details have been avoided. The outline firmly integrates the simple and clear forms, so that the old woman is seen sitting almost as a silhouette before the background which is articulated by a door. As in the early self-portrait (Ill. 2), the immediacy and directness of expression is emphasized by the fact that the drawing looks as though it has been cut out of a larger piece.

Paula Becker spent her first months in Worpswede in seclusion. Before steering her "little ship" out of its "ridiculous isolation"[49] in spring of 1899, she realized with an almost frightening clairvoyance that her development would proceed beyond the Worpswede idyll. "The number of people with whom I can

7
Study of Flowers / Shepherd / Children Among Tree Trunks
c. 1899
Pencil, 26.2 x 40.3 cm
Privately owned

endure speaking about something close to my heart and my nerves will grow smaller and smaller."[50] In spring of 1899 she wrote of several joyous parties in Worpswede, to the social circle of which she now firmly belonged. Apart from Otto Modersohn, Carl Vinnen was the only person who took notice of her as a painter and said to her "kind things about my work".

She read a great deal in those months. It was particularly in reading Nietzsche's "Thus Spake Zarathustra" that she found the moral support she needed to pursue her path consistently.

A journey around Switzerland at the invitation of her aunt Marie Hill enabled her to see herself and Worpswede at a distance and thus to gain the clarity and courage required to state this fact to her family.

On 21 September 1899 (BT 169) she wrote to her sister Milly: "I'm now going through a strange period, perhaps the most serious period in my short life. I can see that my goals will grow further and further distant from yours and that you will disapprove of them more and more. But I must follow them despite everything. I feel everyone taking fright at me, but I must go on. I mustn't turn back. I am striving forwards just as much as you and the others are, but I am doing it in my own mind and in my own skin and according to my own opinion."

In mid-November she began a letter to her parents as follows: "I am going on living my life. There isn't much to write about that, because the very things I would write are those which are not the main point. I don't want to write about the great, living soul of art. It's too delicate a subject for me to write about. So this letter will be no more than an assurance that I am still your old Paula even if something new has happened. And if you don't like this new something, comfort yourselves with the thought that there'll be a time when this new some-

8
Dreeben Seated Facing Right
1899
Charcoal, 43.5 x 75.5 cm
Privately owned

thing is supplanted by something even newer."[51] The letter ends with the words: "Dear God, or whoever else it may be, has caused me to develop like this. Enough of this business!!!"

These letters from Paula, who was now twenty-three, show her consciously and energetically detaching herself from her family. They also show that this detachment does not merely relate to family, professional or artistic matters. Rather, she is very consciously aware of the different nature of her path, which will at the outset make her very lonely. At the same time, her concise use of language expresses that she will pursue this path in all consistency. This requires courage and strength, particularly in a time and in a family in which detachment from traditional ties was less usual than it is today. The subject of the great soul of art, touched upon but deliberately left open in her letter to her father, indicates the value attached to art in the development of Paula Becker's personality.

The year of 1899 ended with a bang. Paula Becker and Marie Bock had exhibited some small landscapes in the Bremen Kunsthalle. The review by Arthur Fitger appeared in the Weser-Zeitung newspaper on 20 December 1899 and was positively scathing. Even considering that critics some hundred years ago wrote with greater emotion and pathos than is usual today, this particular reaction is astonishing and without any factual foundation. "The vocabulary of a clean language is not sufficient to describe the works by the two ladies mentioned, and we do not intend to borrow words from an unclean language."[52]

The acidity of Fitger's criticism is enlightening in two respects as regards the visual arts in Bremen at that time. Firstly, it is aimed against the progressive arts policy of Gustav Pauli, director of the Bremen Kunsthalle in those days. Arthur Fitger himself (born 1840) had since 1869 been working as "a writer who had run off the rails and gone in for painting", but he was also "the oracle of good taste".[53] His art criticisms and essays were widely read both in Bremen and elsewhere. He himself produced hundreds of monumental wall and ceiling paintings of an allegorical and decorative type, and these were prized by a large flock of admirers. A circle of art lovers, which already existed, displayed "a contrast, marked by Hanseatic moderation, to him"[54] and the tendency he represented. In 1823 this circle had founded the Art Association, and in 1849 the Bremen Kunsthalle for art exhibitions including works from outside the region.

There were similar endeavours in other towns of Germany. There, as in Bremen, the public was now given the oportunity to re-learn the history of art, something which was done in a rather leisurely fashion in Bremen, thanks to the solidity of Hanseatic persistence. After all, the pictures by the young Worpswede painters were extremely sceptically received at the exhibition of them in 1895, whereas they were a sensational success when shown at the Munich Glaspalast a little later.

But the Worpswede artists were "outmoded" even then. Impressionist and Postimpressionist painters in France, particularly in Paris, had already set new standards valid for the whole of Europe. Cézanne, van Gogh and Gauguin impressively formulated the language of a type of painting which would, in the new century, defend its laws by other than illusionist principles. Typically, the works of those painters were vehemently rejected at the time and were initially purchased by foreign museums. It was in 1897 that Paul Cézanne's first painting found its way into a public art collection, the Berlin Nationalgalerie.

In 1899, when Gustav Pauli was appointed the first art director of the Bremen Kunsthalle, a new artistic broom swept the city. Pauli released visual art from what had been something of a decorative rôle. Up-to-date artists were now able to display their work in the Kunsthalle. Thus it was that Paula Becker presented some of her pictures to the public of Bremen at the end of the same year. But this process goes beyond local cultural politics. Fitger's criticism expresses a kind of existential disquiet, which may also have induced R. Hamann and C. Einstein to make their peculiar utterances in 1925 and 1926 respectively (see p. 8 ff.)

It is true that we do not know which of Paula Becker's paintings Fitger may have been referring to, but we may assume that the picture SANDPIT ON THE WEYERBERG dating from 1899 (Ill. IV) is closely related and comparable to them.

Fitger's criticism included the following remark[55]: "To anyone who has been seasick, the first square metre of dry land seems like paradise. In the same way, we too may, after passing through that cabinet of studies, be placed in a position where we would declare any other picture to be a masterpiece, even if it were the most ordinary landscape of the kind that is turned out by the dozen."

Fitger was probably disturbed by the fact that these pictures were no longer concerned with reproducing visible nature in a realistic, illusory way, along with atmosphere and breadth, but were aiming at something entirely new: greatly simplified elements of the landscape are combined, tersely and almost roughly, to form a composition whose leading element is the surface of the picture, seen as a surface. In this way Paula Becker had begun to convert into art the knowledge she had gained in Berlin. In these endeavours, she had unwittingly come very close to the Postimpressionist painters Cézanne, van Gogh and Gauguin.

At the time, Paula would certainly have felt comforted, or even honoured, if she had known that Cézanne's paintings had a few years before given rise to very similar reactions.[56] But at that time she did not even know his name.

Pauli wrote: "The constant yelping of the Guardians of Zion, those lovers of kitsch, has always betrayed a good nose for the best of the budding talents. It is not Fitger's disapproval which Paula should have feared, but the possibility of his praise." But these lines were also unable to encourage Paula Becker, because it was not until long after her death that they were printed, on page 14 of his monograph of 1919. During the Christmas of 1899, Pauli wrapped himself in a veil of silence. Only Carl Vinnen, the Worpswede painter, defended the two women painters. In the Christmas Eve issue of the Weser-Zeitung newspaper, he replied by writing: "Oh, it was actually only two women art students in Worpswede, and the only crime they had committed was to exhibit inferior and immature students' works . . ."[57]

This apology may reflect the opinion of friends in Worpswede whose views were probably not so very far removed from Fitger's own. On 17 January 1901, Otto Modersohn wrote in his diary: ". . . I didn't like the pictures she was going to exhibit in Bremen—they weren't intimate, they were too poster-like, and I told her so."[58] Later on, it was the very same Otto Modersohn who—in contrast to the other Worpswede artists—showed understanding for her conception of art.

In any event, Paula Becker was pleased to be able to withdraw from all this unpleasing talk by going on a long-hoped-for trip to Paris, and the time was ripe for such a step. After the period of solitude and quiet in which she had found new clarity, she felt the urge to come to grips with the world once again and use it to develop herself. The only proper place to do this was Paris.

"... like a thunderstorm and a great happening"

Paris, 1900

It was in Paris that Paula once again met Clara Westhoff, her friend from Worpswede. Clara wanted to become a sculptress and was a pupil of Auguste Rodin. For a time the two women shared a studio. Paula registered at the Cola Rossi private academy and, as a sideline, also attended anatomy courses at the State-run École des Beaux Arts.

From the first day of her stay in Paris onwards, she diligently visited museums and exhibitions. She drew copies of her favourite pictures. The week was full of intensive work. On Sundays she went on trips into the surrounding area with Clara, or else she visited people she knew.

She began by having difficulty with the city of Paris itself. "Mankind's entire distress doth touch my soul" is the quotation she gives from Goethe's Faust in a letter to Mr. and Mrs. Modersohn. "There is a great deal of misery here, and much corruption and degeneration. I think that we Germans after all are better people", she states at the end, modifying a poem by J. G. Seume.[59]

A little later, she not only revised her opinion of the French, but joyfully threw herself into the abundant life of Paris. While the preceding years in Worpswede had been a time of internalization and breathing out, she now breathed in and fully absorbed the bustle of the capital. To Paula Becker, the intoxicating variety of Paris, seen against the quiet background of Worpswede, signified the "colourful reflection" of life itself. To Paula Becker, the opposite poles represented by these two realms of experience always had the meaning of an elixir of life, of which she repeatedly had to make use.

Few complete paintings have come down to us from the time of this first stay in Paris. But one of them is the SELF-PORTRAIT, in which Paula Becker depicts herself standing outside her open studio window (Ill. III).

The upright artist's bust is a dark silhouette, seen from slightly below against the brighter façade of a Parisian house. No reproduction, however good, can show the colourful darkness of the human figure. To some slight extent, the face, depicted in reddish-brown hues, is fashioned in three dimensions. Unnecessary details are dispensed with. By glazing and scratching the topmost paint layer, the face is given the structure which this artist always aimed at and later described as the "curly, crisp aspect ...". The ornamental character of the ribbon cut through by the lower edge of the picture lends support to the impression aroused of a two-dimensional and largely symmetrical picture structure. The colour and brightness value of the ribbon—and of the eyes—relate it and them to the surrounding surface.

This surface is articulated into four zones. The upper, horizontal, light-grey strip is to be understood as being the sky. Below this is the turquoise-brown band of the roof, passing behind the head and descending slightly to the right. The surfaces to the sides of the neck contrast strikingly with one another, and this cuts sharply through the symmetry of the picture structure. The beige wall surface on the right includes two tall dark windows, the lower one of which is cut through by the artist's shoulder. This intersection creates in the picture a certain feeling of space, which is though limited to a distinction between the front and the rear. This distinction is cancelled by the surface to the left of the neck, a surface whose internal structure emphasizes the diagonals and makes an almost prismatic impression. This surface, looked at on its own, has the effect of an abstract painting in beige and turquoise tones. There are a few reddish brush strokes establishing a colour relationship with the red of the lips, and also a relationship with the shape of the verticals of the windows and ribbon.

The firmly set structure of the upright format painting, and the perspective created by the onlooker's view from underneath—both these features impart to the onlooker an impression of marked self-confidence and self-awareness, a state of mind which also includes the effort associated with self-assertion. By making the emancipatory gesture contained in this self-portrait, Paula Becker was reflecting firstly her personal situation during these months in Paris, and secondly the general situation of a woman artist around the turn of the century.[60]

Paula Becker came upon a triptych by the painter Cottet, who is almost forgotten today, and also found some works by other unknown artists. She described the experience as important to her art.[61] We do not find in her letters the names of those artists who should have exercised a magical attraction upon her. This is probably attributable to two causes: firstly the presumed incompleteness of the writings she left to posterity, and secondly her peculiar way of coming to terms with artistic styles that were foreign to her. It seems that when in Paris she began, and repeatedly continued, to seek things she knew and was familiar with. G. Busch observes on this subject: "It is not a rare occurrence for movements and developments to be brought about by figures of second or third rank—either in general, or else in respect of individual recipients whom these figures affect as if they were catalysts, by merely passing on energies originating from farther away."[62]

But it is also possible that her encounters with works of art took place on differing planes of experience. This would mean that when she arrived in Paris her thoughts and feelings were in tune with works in Cottet's style. But at a deeper, unconscious level her artistic development had already proceeded much further. This is borne out by the above quotations from her Berlin period, where she speaks of "Schauen" ("looking"), and by some of her works, such as those which met with Fitger's opposition.

This is the most probable explanation for the shock she must have experienced when she discovered pictures by the painters who had reached the same stage as she. She was evidently deeply affected by these encounters. Seen in this way, they were not included in her letters or diary entries, but instead became a direct part of her own artistic work.

It was Clara Westhoff's notes from a much later period that tell us of their encounter with Cézanne.[63] One day, the two young women were on a visit to Vollard, in whose art dealer's shop there were many paintings facing the wall. Paula turned them round one by one, and was enthusiastic about what she saw.

They were by Cézanne. At that time the two of them did not even know his name. But Paula must have realized that she was on the right track artistically. It was not until much later, a few weeks before her death, that she reminded her friend of this experience in a letter: "In the last few days I have been thinking a great deal about Cézanne and how he was one of the three or four painters whose effect on me was like that of a thunderstorm and a great happening. Do you remember Vollard's shop in 1900?" (BT 475).

In the works of Cézanne, van Gogh and Gauguin—to name only the most important artists—, what was the new feature that made them the fathers of modern painting? To explain the qualitatively new feature of painting at the turn of the century, together with the intellectual background which became effective in that painting, we must go back somewhat further.

Since the Renaissance, painters had been endeavouring to create true-to-nature reproductions of visible reality. The most important artistic element was the draughtsman's linear perspective, discovered in Italy in the first few decades of the 15th century.[64] Its appearance marks a decisive step, rich in consequences, in the further development of Western painting.

Perspective is that technique in drawing which enables the artist to reproduce external space with a seemingly photographic exactness. But it is an illusion because it pretends to the onlooker that there is a space which, to him, does not exist. This is because perspective abstracts the onlooker from the mental and physiological processes of visual perception. For example, it tacitly gives the impression that we see with a single, immobile eye and that the physiological image produced on the retina is not concave, but flat. Thus it does not take into account the distortions at the edge of the visual image. It also tricks us into thinking that the space perceived by the eye is infinite and homogenous. But these alleged properties of space are not really seen by the eye, but are introduced by us into the visual image as ideas which we have learned. Thus it is as if the draughtsman's perspective were converting the psycho-physiological space into a mathematical construction.

Erwin Panofsky explained perspective as a "symbolic form"[65], because it is "a concrete expression of what had at the same time been achieved in the fields of the theory of knowledge and of natural philosophy [...]". But it was rational awareness that was the agent operating in all these developments and expressive forms. This awareness became so dominant in the further course of history that it finally determined Western man's perception of himself. Descartes found the applicable formula for this in his phrase: "Cogito, ergo sum."

A transformation of style in art—and not only in visual art—is much more than a rapidly changing fashionable phenomenon. The history of styles in painting is also a history of seeing. Seeing, like any other form of perception, is not only a physiological but also a mental process. For this reason the development of painting can also be interpreted as a manifestation of the development of human awareness: "Style is one's view of existence, put in a specific form. If style changes, then vision and insight changed first."[66]

An enormous abundance of new possibilities, relating to both form and content, was opened up to painting by the development of the drawn linear perspective: light and shade effects, instantaneous records of seemingly flowing movements, mobility on the time scale with optional access to past, present, and future (the latter being seen as in a vision). All of this called upon this painter to reproduce the variety of human life as a visual illusion and to give to painting a wider variety of different meanings than ever before.

But this immense enrichment of the world of painting could only be achieved on one condition, the price of which was included in considerations on the subject: psychological and physiological variety had to be reduced to a mathematically constructed system. Thus, after the use of perspective had enjoyed an initial triumph, there were tendencies, in Mannerism, to break away from the restrictions imposed by the need to create an illusion of depth in a picture.

Once the 19th century had arrived at a sober, scientific view of the world, the field of painting shook off, effectively and one by one, the idealistic burdens which by now were mere ballast. Now that painting was liberated, it achieved its own formal regularity. This resulted firstly in effects based on the pure visual nature of the world, and secondly in "l'art pour l'art", in which art merely signifies itself.

The 19th century was a time in which many currents of the visual arts were developing both simultaneously and successively to one another. The Realists (Courbet and Millet in France, and later Leibl in Germany) were closely related to the development of the sciences and industrialization. From the middle of the century onwards, the Realists had been attempting to depict visible reality—and only visible reality—while excluding everything felt or known and, in particular, without including any idealizing tendencies. Their aim was not to show sublime meanings and display them in theatrical style, but to describe exactly the everyday life of workers and peasants. The colour of an object was conceived as being the surface of things, and the eye now scanned that surface with complete objectivity. But this conception is yet another "idea which has always been projected into pure seeing and has always been known to be there along with the purely optical element"[67].

The Impressionists observed the seeing process with greater exactitude than the Realists. For the Impressionists, the only matter of importance was the constantly changing sensual perceptions, brought about by momentary lighting conditions and subjective circumstances.[68] So they no longer depicted the objects themselves, but rather the coloured stimuli of light which come from those objects and hit the retina: this is the coloured web between object and brain. By using small dots and strokes to build up their coloured surfaces in the pure colours of the spectrum, which are complementary colours, they created a kind of "optical skin"[69], in which colour became the sparkling bearer of atmospheric light. In this way they capture the fleeting beauty of a moment by depicting accidental details of nature and light. By using this technique based on a new experience of seeing, the Impressionists liberated colour from its task of only representing the surface of things. Paintings were created in a new and bold colourfulness, no longer tied down by any previous knowledge or idea concerning an object.

The artists who embraced the new mode of painting experienced it as a liberating power. Free artistic development had long been inhibited by the incrustations of Academism, which was fed by sentimentality and photographic accuracy of reproduction. But art now created new paths for itself and became incredibly productive, so that painting in the decades around the turn of the century changed rapidly and fanned out in many different directions.

But when, as is possible today, Impressionist art is looked at from the viewpoint of abstract and non-representational painting, then Impressionism is also "a maximum advance into a dead end"[70], because although it liberated colour from any particular object, this object continued to be present in an intermediate state between existence and non-existence, and was also tied to an illusionist impression of depth created by perspective. What is more, colour—if examined closely—had not really been liberated and thus allowed to achieve its own strength, but had been tied to its bearer, the sunlight which lit things up and cast shadows.

It was left to the Post-Impressionists, who were the generation of painters following the Impressionists, to achieve the complete liberation of colour, and along with it the liberation of the other tools used in pictures, such as form and line. This made the Post-Impressionists the fathers of modern art. But anyone who came to grips creatively with the artistic problems which were topical at the time had to deal with the principles of Impressionistic painting. Only in this way was it possible to reap the fruits of this development in painting and at the same time to escape from the "dead end".[71]

Paul Cézanne was the first painter who consistently put into effect the experienced gained by pure seeing. He released himself from the manner of depiction which used a central perspective, and he painted pictures that take into account the psycho-physiological processes of visual perception by using, for example, more than one vanishing point and more than one line of vision. Cézanne was also aware that purely objective depiction, which excludes feelings and psychological processes, is not possible. Thus, to him, the artistic process does not mean a reproduction of nature as found in the world outside, and does not mean the creation of an illusion, but means a new creation "in parallel with nature"[72]. Painting a picture became an act of creation in itself. He took the colours liberated by the Impressionists, and the shapes suggested by things occurring in nature, and used them to create compositions in which the surface of the picture, seen as a surface, was both the point of departure and the point of reference.

The importance which Cézanne attached to preventing rational thought from intervening in the intuitive artistic process can be seen from a conversation he had with Joachim Gasquet: "What lies behind nature? Nothing at all, perhaps. And perhaps everything. So I clasp together these wandering hands of mine. I take up these hues of colour, these gradations, from the right, left, here, there, everywhere, and I tie them down and bring them together. They form lines and turn into objects, rocks, trees, without my thinking about it. They take on a volume . . . my canvas clasps its hands together. It does not fluctuate. It is true, it is compact, it is full. But if I show the slightest weakness, and especially . . . if I think while I am painting, if I myself intervene, then everything collapses and is lost."[73]

The same conversation between Cézanne and Gasquet contains remarks whch confirm that he too regards as valid the knowledge gained by Fiedler, consisting of thoughts concerning an expanded possession of reality achieved through "pure seeing". At the same time, that conversation announces the emergence of a form of awareness which Jean Gebser describes as "non-perspective" or "integral" and which he characterizes as being a form of awareness belonging to a new era. Cézanne: "Art is a harmony paralleling nature . . . The painter is on the same level as his art, if he does not intervene of his own accord. His whole faculty of wishing must be silent. He must let all the voices of prejudice grow silent within him, he must forget, be quiet and be a complete echo. The nature of the world outside, and that of the world within (he struck himself on the forehead), must penetrate one another in order to endure and to live, a life that is half human and half divine, the life of art. The landscape reflects itself, becomes human, imagines itself within me. I externalize it and record it on my canvas. You were talking to me about Kant recently. I may be talking nonsense, but it seems to me that I represent the subjective awareness of this landscape and that my canvas represents its objective awareness."

In these words there are tendencies to be heard which point to a view of the "world with nothing opposite it"[74]. This is a view which does not split the world up into a dualism of object/subject, and also does not break time down into past, present and future, but overcomes these sub-distinctions by virtue of the "freedom of the ego"[75]. Thus existence, being permanent present time, shines through all things.

The place occupied by Cézanne in the history of art is characterized by the fact that he provided the liberated pictorial means which are not restricted to a representational interpretation of the world but which, by operating solely through themselves, express a reality which goes beyond pure materiality. Kandinsky described this expanded reality as "the spiritual in art", while Willi Baumeister referred to it as "the unknown in art".

And what did Paula Becker do?

When she came to Paris in early 1900, she was, as we have seen, prepared by her own strength to absorb by osmosis, as it were, the artistic developments taking place at this focal point of European art. She too felt that it was necessary to come to terms with Impressionism. She thought that the conception of nature found in Monet's pictures was "superficial"[76].

As is customary in art history, her work was, and still is, compared with the work of other painters, especially Cézanne, and is measured by the standards of that work. Some reminiscences of contemporary artists' works are certainly to be found in her pictures. Paula Becker did not work in a vacuum. She needed stimulation. In the final analysis, comparisons with others artists contribute little to an understanding of her painting, because they do not lead on to the specific features of her own art. She always only absorbed what had already been prepared within her, and the result was her own works showed a "resonance" with others[77]. As regards her relationship with Cézanne, it may be observed that the psychological and spiritual process of perception, and the manner in which the items perceived are transformed into art, are not dependent on Cézanne, but proceed in parallel with him. Paula Becker learned certain things from Cézanne in the field of art, chiefly consistency and severity of composition. It is in her still lifes that her style comes closest to his. Let it be emphasized at this point that her entire artistic development meant that the results she achieved were diametrically opposite to those of Cézanne: while Cézanne arrived at a dematerialization and immateriality of all things, Paula Becker followed the path of making the world appear more and more compact.[78]

The development of her personality took an important step forwards during this period in Paris. She became aware of her womanliness. Her diary entries allow us an insight into how she experienced this and dealt with it.

She perceives the newness around her and it puts her in a mood of near-euphoria. "And then I experience the dawning humanity in me. I am becoming a woman. The child begins to recognize life, woman's final purpose, and awaits life's fulfilment. And life will be beautiful, wonderful. And I walk along the boulevards, encountering crowds of people, and a voice within me calls out: 'Of all

9
GARDEN
1900/02
Charcoal, 41.5 x 39.5 cm
Sketch-book VI, sheet 2

of you, not one, not a single one, possesses anything as beautiful as what still lies before me.' And then the voice calls: 'When will it come? Soon?' And then art speaks and wants two more serious uninterrupted years of work. Life is serious, full of content, and beautiful."[79] The high spirits of the mid-April days are followed by deep sadness towards the end of the month. She knows perfectly well that this is the maturing process she has already perceived, and she trustingly allows this process to happen. She feels, in the depths of her, the flowing of a river she calls the "Styx"; it is the river which, in Greek mythology, separates the earthly world from the underworld.

By that time, external events were taking a course which permitted the internal events to manifest themselves outwardly.

The International Exhibition began in Paris in May. Paula was excited by it and asked Otto Modersohn to come to Paris along with his wife and their Worpswede friends. Her friends finally agreed to her request. They went to Paris, leaving behind the dangerously ill Helene Modersohn. Hardly had they begun to enjoy the International Exhibition when Otto Modersohn heard the news of the death of his wife. He immediately returned.

"Casting the nets..."

Worpswede, 1900–1903

Paula followed Otto in late June 1900. She set up a small studio in Ostendorf near Worpswede, in the house of a peasant named Brünjes. After she had come into contact with the city of Paris, there now followed a phase of withdrawal. Here, in this quietude, she decided to strip away "all the vainglory which the city brought with it and to make" of herself "a true human being and a sensitive woman"[80]. But external circumstances now came to beset her again: the funds she had so unexpectedly received three years before had been used up, and her father was once again urging her at last to take up a post as a governess. But a different fate had already been quietly prepared for her.

Paula was now twenty-four years old. She now fell ill. She had led an intense life in Paris, and may also have been affected by the unreasonable demand that she should work as a governess, a demand which, although certainly justified from her father's point of view, was hard to reconcile with her calling as a painter. As a result she became completely exhausted, and the doctor ordered her to stay in bed. It was on 26 June 1900 that she wrote in her diary those famous sentences to which a prophetic significance was later attributed when her early death was known (BT 231):

"When I was painting today, some ideas came to me and I want to write them down for my dear ones. I know that I shall not live very long. But is that sad? Is a festival better if it lasts for longer? And my life is a festival, a brief and intense festival." She then describes how her sensual perception is becoming more delicate "as if I were to absorb everything, everything, in the few years that will be given me". Then she continues: "And if love blossoms for me before I pass away, and if I have painted three good pictures by then, I shall be glad to pass away with flowers in my hands and in my hair."

Are these words a genuine premonition of death, seven years before her actual death? Or are they the expression of feelings which, because they were experienced in an hour of weakness, need not be taken entirely seriously?[81] It is difficult, and perhaps impossible, for us outsiders, born in a later era, to see these words in the right perspective. They came to her in a state of heightened intuition while she was painting. Whatever the case, a year and a half later she gave a very exact description of the tomb she wanted for herself[82], which was intended to look very different from the one later built for her by Berhard Hoetger.[83] She also mentioned the brevity of life in a poem she wrote. Let us not forget her very close encounter with death at the age of ten. Being a consciously living woman, Paula Modersohn-Becker certainly deeply experienced the truth of Goethe's words

Und so lang du das nicht hast,
Dieses: Stirb und Werde!
Bist du nur ein trüber Gast
Auf der dunklen Erde...

("You must have this to hand, / This: Die, and Be! If not / A cheerless guest you'll stand / Upon the Earth's dark plot...")

But she was not lonely in those weeks, for Otto Modersohn was free and often came and saw her to read to her and cheer her up. Thus it was that that loving relationship arose in which Paula was to experience her newly awakened womanliness. At the same time the problem of how she was to make a living was solved by her ties with Otto Modersohn. External circumstances had once again adapted themselves to inner necessities.

A few weeks after this low point, she was once again in the best of health and overjoyed with it: "It is going to go on for a long time after all. I am healthy and strong and alive. Hail!" she jubilantly wrote in her diary.[84] On 12 August, she and Clara Westhoff, standing on the Worpswede church tower and overcome by the beautiful view, sounded the fire signal for an overabundant late summer and autumn. The villagers gathered, expecting a large fire. The pastor, who was annoyed, put a stop to this "public mischief" and ordered the two women to atone for their deed by producing a work of art, considering that they did not have the funds to pay a fine. Clara Westhoff fashioned the heads of putti on the columns of the Worpswede church, and Paula Becker painted meadow flowers underneath.[85]

The climax of that period was when Paula became engaged to Otto Modersohn on 12 September. They kept it secret at first, because it was not long since Helene Modersohn had died.[86]

In Worpswede itself, the various artists had become largely estranged from one another.[87] But Heinrich Vogeler and Otto Modersohn had established a closer mutual relationship. They formed the core of a small circle which often liked to meet socially, usually in Vogeler's "Barkenhoff". The "family", as they called themselves, included Heinrich Vogeler and his Martha Schröder, Otto Modersohn and Paula Becker, Clara Westhoff, Marie Bock and Paula's sister Milly. The arrival of the two poets Carl Hauptmann and Rainer Maria Rilke lent a romantic gloss to these gatherings. A trip to Hamburg, to visit the Kunsthalle and the theatre, was the high point of their activities.

A deep friendship arose between Rilke and Paula Becker. This was later darkened when Rilke married Paula's friend Clara Westhoff and made Clara's life a permanent "hour of remembrance".[88] But Paula Backer still enjoyed listening to the poet using a language never heard before to sound a new chord within her. Rilke recorded one of his visits to her in his diary as follows[89]:

"Then I was in the lily studio. There was tea awaiting me. A good and pure feeling of mutuality in both talk and silence. Evening came on in wondrous fashion; the talk was of Tolstoy, death, Georges Rodenbach, Hauptmann's 'Peace Festival', life, beauty in all experience, the ability to die and the wish to die, eternity and why we feel related to eternal souls. Of so many things that extend beyond the present hour and beyond ourselves. Everything became mysterious. The clock struck the hour much too insistently and made a great noise in moving very loudly to and fro among our conversations. Her hair was of Florentine gold. Her voice had folds in it like silk. I had never seen her looking so delicate and slender in her white girlishness."

IX
Children with Lanterns
1901
Cardboard, 38.5 x 52 cm
Stuttgart, privately owned

X
Otto Modersohn
GARDEN WITH GLASS BALL AND ELSBETH
Dated at lower left: 28.VI.03
Oil on cardboard, 41.5 x 58 cm
Fischerhude, Otto-Modersohn-Museum

XI
ELSBETH IN GARDEN BESIDE GLASS BALL
c. 1902
Oil distemper on cardboard, 35.7 x 35.7 cm
Privately owned

XII
Girl in Front of Window
1902/1903
Slate, 39.3 x 49.5 cm
Privately owned

XIII
Portrait of a Sick Girl
1901
Oil distemper on canvas and cardboard, 35 x 33 cm
Münster, Westphalian State Museum of Art and Cultural History

XIV
Mother Suckling Her Child
c. 1903
Oil on canvas, 70 x 58.8 cm
Hanover, State Museum of Lower Saxony

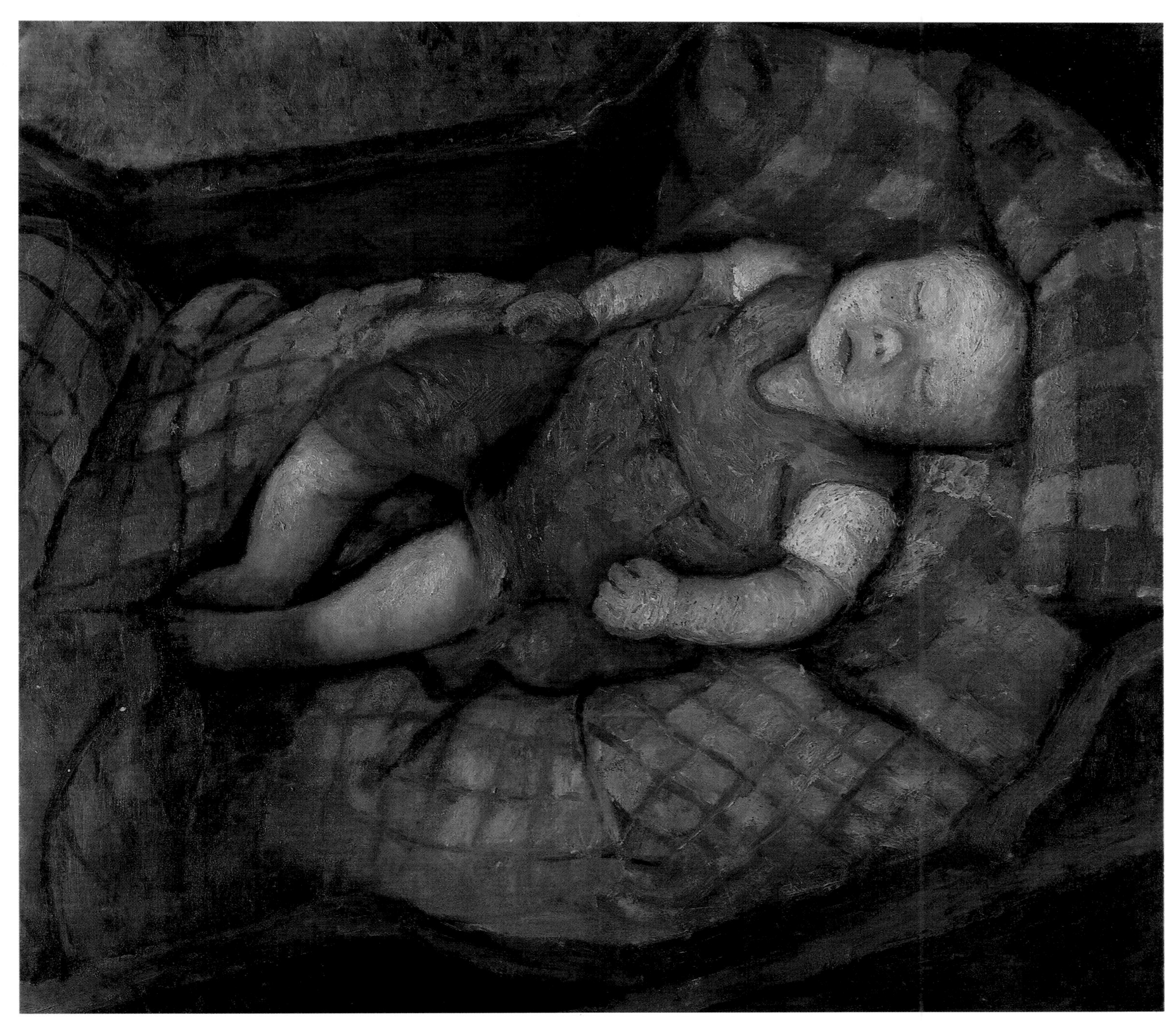

XV
Sleeping Child
c. 1904
Oil on canvas, 62.5 x 69.5 cm
Privately owned

XVI
PORTRAIT OF CLARA RILKE-WESTHOFF
1905
Oil distemper on canvas
52 x 36.8 cm
Hamburg, Kunsthalle

With unexpected suddenness, Rilke left for Berlin in early October. Paula wrote to him there to inform him of her engagement.

Paula Becker painted some sixty landscape studies in those weeks of most intense personal experience between August and December 1900. The term "study"[90] refers to her attitude towards her landscape paintings. She used it for a long time to refer to completed paintings on other subjects: she thought of herself as a learner all her life. The numerous paintings with birch trees in or in front of a landscape were regarded by her as exercises in how to handle colour, shape and composition.

The Worpswede painters, Fritz Overbeck and—as was natural—Otto Modersohn, prompted her to paint landscapes. The two of them often worked standing before the same subject.

Her concern with this topic was an echo of her deep experience of landscapes and of nature as a whole. The gushingly romantic way in which Paula Becker expressed this experience in her diary is never found in her paintings, as can be seen from the SANDPIT ON THE WEYERBERG dating from 1899 (Ill. IV). It is precisely here that she differs from the other Worpswede painters, including Otto Modersohn, because they strive after atmospheric, lyrical or pathetic glimpses of the moorland expanses, whereas she constructs her paintings from individual, greatly simplified elements, forming them into compositions in which the surfaces are emphasized. Eliminating all subjective feelings, she reduces the landscapes to mere visibility. "I'm drawing and painting a great deal," she wrote to her parents from Norway on 20 June 1898 (BT 131). "First of all I addressed myself to the landscape. But the colours and shapes of the landscape make such a divinely simple impression that years of study would be needed to reproduce this simplicity without any roughness. So I've now painted the little calf [...]"

The paint employed itself contributes to the impression of sobriety. Following Otto Modersohn's suggestion, she usually used the "Wurmsche Temperafarbe" distemper, which yields a matt painted surface. She sometimes used oils to work over the distemper paintings. The impression made by her paintings is often falsified when they are reproduced, not only because the colours of the reproductions are often different and too strong, but also because of their silken or gleaming surface. She painted most of her pictures on thin, green to brownish cardboard, using a simple white chalk background.[91]

The lower half of WORPSWEDE LANDSCAPE, which dates from 1900 (Ill. VI), is built up of clayey green and brown hues. Spontaneous-looking brush strokes give the coloured areas structure, contrast them with one another and provide the most important elements of the landscape: bare little trees, hayricks, a vermilion house between bushes above an olive-green strip. The bright grey sky, lightly worked over in red, takes up more than half the height of the picture. A single tree, standing right of centre in the picture and leaning slightly to the left, cuts through almost the entire surface of the picture. The picture's upper edge cuts through the crown of the tree. The green of its leaves, and some patches on the meadow, are darkened in Prussian blue. In the lower zone, one of the tree's twigs, together with some branches of a small tree behind it, ornamentally surrounds a haycock.

A striking feature of this, as of most, landscape paintings by Paula Modersohn-Becker is its sombre colouring. One reason for this is the colours of the Worpswede landscape. But it is also the expression of her experience and her basic artistic conception of sunlight and shade, of light and colour. Writing from Paris to Mr. and Mrs. Modersohn in 1900[92], she stated: "The earth is much too bright for me when the sun is shining. It is then that I would like all the colours to be deeper, more mellow. This brightness really irritates me." A little later, she wrote of a painting by Jean Pierre[93]: "This picture has a little corner which expresses what I am striving after: a deep, coloured, luminous strength in the half-light, a coloured glow in the shade, a glow although there is no sun, as in autumn and spring in Worpswede, a bright blue sky, large, white balls of cloud and no sun." A year later she had become reconciled with the sun: "I think I am even gaining a relationship with the sun. Not with the sun that divides everything and puts shadows everywhere and pulls the picture into a thousand pieces, but with the sun that broods and makes things grey and weighty and links them all in this grey weightiness, so that they may all become one."[94] This statement means that her position was the exact opposite to that of the Impressionists, who tried to use sparkling colours to capture the atmospheric, illuminating, shadow-casting sunlight. In Paula Becker's landscape paintings, the sunlight seems to enter the material of the paint itself and to give it an inner luminous strength of its own. This liberates the colours, enabling them to achieve their own natural effects, the bearer of which is the coloured brush stroke (cf. van Gogh) or the coloured surface (cf. Gauguin).

Paul Gauguin had used the following formulation in about 1890: "Look at the Japanese artists with their coloured woodcuts. They use colours merely as a combination of harmonies. I too would like to stay as far away as possible from everything that makes an illusionist impression. I am inclined to suppress shadows, because they are the illusionist element of the sun. But if shadow is necessary as a form fitting into your composition, then that is another matter. But do not regard yourself as the slave of shadow."[95] In Paula Modersohn-Becker's painting of the WORPSWEDE LANDSCAPE in the Lower Saxony Landesgalerie (Ill. VI), the lightly indicated shadows are a "necessary form".

As regards the artistic conception of her landscapes, Paula Becker seems to have been closer to her contemporaries Gauguin and van Gogh than to Cézanne. On this subject, Otto Modersohn wrote in his letter to Pauli (1919)[96]: "She was not interested in achieving Cézanne's division of surfaces, his lights and shades, his lack of concern for the object or for how the surface was divided up among the separate things. I had purchased some German photographs of Cézanne's landscapes, but they were incomprehensible to her, and indeed they had to be incomprehensible by the standards of her endeavours at that time."

Later on, Paula Modersohn-Becker used brighter and more brilliant colours in her landscapes too, such as the painting BIRCHTREES IN AUTUMN dating from 1900 (Ill. V).

Warmly luminous dabs of paint and black thrusting brush-strokes, placed above clayey, interrelated painted surfaces, lend the painting a structure which makes one think at first of "façon hachée", the broken-up manner used by the Impressionists. But the paint has its own colourful force at all points, so that the illusion of a depth bathed in atmospheric light or of an "optical skin" does not arise.

The study of the WORPSWEDE LANDSCAPE described above is at the Landesgalerie in Hanover (Ill. VI) and has an astonishing peculiarity which it shares with some other landscape paintings and still lifes by this artist: the picture itself stimulates the process of looking at it, and makes this a conscious process.

The relative proportions of the individual elements of the landscape, the diagonals in the inner structure of the lower surface, the way in which the brightness values are gradated towards the top of the picture, and the tree which cuts through the whole height of the picture—all this permits the onlooker to use his habits of seeing to associate the picture with a feeling of depth. But the sky with its thick, dully shining brightness is far towards the front of the picture, almost on its surface. The clash of the sky with the landscape is so designed that the impression of the sky being near the front is further intensified. Sometimes the painter rubs the contrasting colours into the picture so as to form indefinite transitions, and sometimes she places the darker colour of the landscape above the brightness of the sky. But she often finishes by putting the bright paint above the darker, as as here been done around the large tree. In doing so she actually emphasizes the contrast by hollowing out the dark form, using the paint which has been specially brightened up for this purpose.

Starting from the lower area of the picture, the onlooker sees a landscape which lies under a broad sky and leads into the depths of the picture. But hardly has he begun to do so when he is forced, in looking at the large tree and the grey sky to the right of it, to cease this process and to withdraw the association in order to be able to go into the picture once again, looking with greater hesitation and awareness this time.

Anyone looking at the painting DITCH ON THE MOOR (c. 1900/02; Ill. VII) will have a similar experience.

The horizon line is near the top of this picture. The landscape is opened up, occupying nearly the whole surface of the picture. The diagonal of the canal crossing the moor, the way it narrows towards the top, the gradation of the colour and size of the landscape elements as they approach the sky zone—all this gives rise to the idea of a certain, though not very great, depth in the picture. Bushes, and—in immensely differentiated nuances of colour—the blue of the sky and the grey of the clouds, are seen reflected in the ditch in the moor. The colour of the clouds reflected in the ditch corresponds to the colour of the area of sky at the top edge of the picture, and this strengthens the impression of flatness seen in the picture.

After one has looked at the picture for some time, the canal through the moor, with its luminous colours, seems to detach itself from the darkness of its banks and to become an independent, symbolic form of its own. The onlooker may regard this form as a negative form between two positive areas of canal-bank or—by way of a reverse interpretation—as a positive form between two dark negative forms.

In summer 1907 the mature Paula Becker felt induced to write the following to Bernhard Hoetger (BT 473):

"I wanted to defeat Impressionism by trying to forget it. In this way I myself was defeated. We must work with the Impressionism which we have come to terms with and digested."

In early 1901 Paula Becker went to Berlin for two months to learn to cook. On her birthday she received a letter from her mother who impressively demonstrated to her the duties both of a wife and of an artist's wife[97]: "It is your duty to be completely absorbed in your future husband and to devote yourself to him in complete accordance with his particular characteristics and his wishes, always to have his welfare in mind and not to let yourself be guided by selfish thoughts. [...] It is a wife's task to be lenient in her married life, to keep

10
Otto Modersohn Reading at a Table
c. 1904
Charcoal over pencil, 24.3 x 29.4 cm
Bremen, privately owned

her eye open for all that is good and fine about her husband, and to view his little weaknesses through a reducing glass. [...] So far as I know him, he may be too good-natured and, being an artist, he may also be so impractical that he will give you a completely free hand and will allow himself to be guided by you in many ways, but you must then be all the more moderate, and remember that thrift is the best form of gain. [...] You must have more regard to your little stepdaughter than to your own wishes. Otto loves the child and would certainly later regret having done anything that might, in the opinion of experts, be harmful to the child."

She herself reflected on the preparations for marriage in a letter to her future husband, dated 6 March: "It's strange that it is we women who have to bear the trials right from the beginning of marriage onwards. You men are allowed to stay just as you are. Well, I don't hold that against you, because I like you so much as you are. But that's probably why the male character is generally stronger than the female character, being more interrelated and more of an integrated whole. By this I don't mean us two particularly, for I too think that I am an integrated whole; but I'm referring to men and women generally" (BT 294).

For Paula, Otto Modersohn was on the one hand a sensitive artist with whom she sought close co-operation, but on the other hand he was a soft, emotional and naive person—"simple and childlike, and boyish in his happiness. As a reflective person, I have a devout and humble regard for this simple soul," she wrote to her aunt Marie Hill.[98]

Otto Modersohn's relationship with Paula Becker, who was a cheerful person full of the joy of living, was a particular gift to him, because his years of marriage to his first wife had been marked by her serious illness and the constant danger that she might die. On 26 November 1900[99], he noted in his diary: "What happiness it is to me that I have found my Paula. This is a happiness I cannot prize highly enough. She is just the kind of girl I need. [...] Paula is a

11
Otto Modersohn
Paula Modersohn-Becker Painting
7 September 1901
Privately owned

mature, rich-minded girl with a hundred different interests, with true, real, higher needs, with a cheerful mind full of the joy of being alive. When I am with her I often feel as if I were growing wings, as if I were being unburdened; everything in me is enlivened and becomes so light and cheerful. How valuable that is to me! I have a definite tendency to be serious and pensive. I am often like that when I am alone. Paula is a true comfort to me there: she cheers, refreshes, enlivens and rejuvenates."

The wedding was held on 25 May 1901, not in the Zionskirche church in Worpswede, but at her father's sickbed—he died in November of the same year.

Paula immediately made energetic arrangements for her new life. She knew that she would need to divide up her day strictly if she was to perform her duties as a wife and as Elsbeth's mother and at the same time fulfil her function as an artist. Otto Modersohn had intentionally also married Paula as an artist, and he supported her wherever he could. A maid relieved her of much of the housework. But disrupting scenes repeatedly occurred, and all members of the family suffered from them.

Paula Modersohn spent the first years of her marriage to Otto Modersohn in happiness, but she was nevertheless to learn "that marriage does not make one happier. It takes away the illusion on which my whole being formerly rode: the illusion that there is a sister soul. When married, I feel twice as much as before that I am not being understood, because the whole of life before marriage amounted to finding a being that understood. And might it not be better without this illusion, might it not be better to look at a great solitary truth eye to eye? I am writing this in my kitchen housekeeping book on Easter Sunday 1902, while sitting in my kitchen and cooking roast veal."[100] She accepted solitude because it reveals "certain depths and shallows of which two people together are not so aware"[101].

When they were living together, a time of joint artistic work began.[102] Otto Modersohn may have begun by regarding Paula as a kind of pupil—he was eleven years older than her and a recognized painter. Moreover, Paula felt that she was a beginner, and she put all her trust in her husband's guidance. She painted mainly landscapes at this time. They often both stood painting the same subject, so that the resultant pictures strongly resembled one another.

But the similar results the two of them arrived at were achieved at completely different periods of their personal and artistic development. These results have differing significances in the development of the two artists. The paintings of Otto Modersohn, right to the very last, belong to the 19th century, although he died in 1943. His landscapes are atmospheric and comparatively realistic. At the same time they show some Impressionist elements in their colour and handwriting. He liked small, intimate things. He had an invigorating, but at the same time muting, effect on Paula. She reduced her range of colours and preferred to use earthy, clayey colours.

It was quite soon, in early July 1902, that Otto Modersohn confessed to himself in his diary that his pupil Paula had become a colleague to be taken seriously[103]:

"My Paula is a fine lass. An artist through and through. [. . .] I cannot keep up with her at the moment. [. . .] This is tremendously good for me. It rouses me. 'That little lassie painting better than you, come off it, some chance.' I'll really have to begin now, boy. I'm keeping my eyes open. It'll be a race." Two days later, he summed up with brilliant brevity what painting meant to Paula:

12
Children With Lanterns
1901
Charcoal, 17.6 x 22 cm
Privately owned

"In brief, painting is seeing, feeling, doing. [...] Ever since I began thinking like this after looking at Paula's study[104], I have felt harmony and chords everywhere. Nothing is separated—everything is connected. Air and light, the great unifiers. [...] Paula is my comrade. Paula is a genius of a woman [...]."[105]

A year later, Paula was to write to her husband from Paris some lines that show how a picture is made: "One of your expressions is: 'One gets a feeling that is has all started happening.' When you're painting a picture, the first thing is that you should express the full strength of this feeling. You must know all the means of doing this off pat: the technique, the paint and the great form. These are your means, and the aim is to create your compositions so as to make them into pictures."[106]

One composition for which she knew all the means "off pat" is the picture Children with Lanterns, 1901 (Ill. IX).

A group of children of different ages is walking along in the gathering twilight, carrying Chinese lanterns. The scene has been transformed into a two-dimensional composition.

The shadowy figures of the children have been reduced to very simple surfaces. But some precisely observed details enable the onlooker to re-experience the scene. Loving care has been employed in reproducing the way in which the lanterns are being waved, and the excitement with which two smaller children are looking into their lantern.

The cool steely glow of the sky is a key element in the composition. It causes warm tones, orange and red, to be chosen for the other colours. From the darkness of green and earthy hues there grows a rich coloured harmony of broken browns and blues. These grow warmer and brighter on their way up the picture until they merge with the luminous surfaces of the lanterns. The coloured heart of the picture is in its right-hand lower quarter, where the lantern and the two small children are to be found.

The arrangement of the surfaces follows the upwards movement. Comparatively large rectangles are seen rising up from the ground. The round shapes of

13
Boy Leaning Against Tree
c. 1903
Chalk, 22.3 x 16.8 cm
Hamburg Kunsthalle

the arms and heads alternate with one another against the blue of the sky. The upwards tendency culminates in the lanterns. The brightest lantern, that on the right, is even pushed up out of the picture. The large and small, rectangular and round surfaces placed rhythmically in front of, above and beside one another make the children appear to be huddled close together.

The brightness of the individual coloured surfaces is finely gradated. But the luminous strength of the colours does not lie in the illuminating shining force of the candles, but in the paint itself. As in the landscape studies discussed above, the colours have been liberated so that they can achieve their effect independently of the object depicted.

The figure crouching at the bottom left is seen to be gleaming for no particular reason. The compositional sketch (Ill. 12) for the painting (Ill. IX) has a standing figure in this position. In the completed painting, Paula Modersohn-Becker has evidently altered this motif for a particular reason: it is now practically intended to catch the onlooker's eye. Starting from this figure, his gaze, moving up and down, wanders towards the right of the picture, rises to the edge of the picture where the bright right-hand lantern is, and finally stops at the red lantern below. This is also where the movement of the group, a stumbling rather than a walking movement, comes to a standstill.

In this composition, Paula Modersohn-Becker has found a language of forms which, despite being tied to an objective representation, anticipates the pictorial ideas of Paul Klee.

In the first years of her marriage, Paula Modersohn-Becker painted not only landscapes, but also many portraits of children: children alone or with animals, in the open fields, leaning against trees, playing together in groups, brothers and sisters... Over sixty works on this subject survive from the year 1902 alone (see Ill. 13).

This artist had a close relationship with children. She lovingly observed them arriving and growing up in the villagers' cradles. The Rilkes and the Vogelers had also had additions to their families. She herself suffered more and more from her childlessness. She had become a loving mother to Elsbeth, Otto Modersohn's daughter from his first marriage. She celebrated unforgettably merry festivals with Elsbeth and her friends. She "understood how to be a child among children".[107]

The portraits of children by Paula Modersohn-Becker reflect the change in ideas about children around the turn of the century.[108] For centuries children had been looked at from the adult's point of view, and in pictures they had often been dressed up as representatives of claims to social standing. In the 19th century, under the influence of Jean Jacques Rousseau's writings, the child was seen more as a child, but was often prettified and placed in rather idyllic, genre-type surroundings (as in the works of Hans Thoma and F. von Uhde). At around the turn of the century, a child's situation began to be seen a little more realistically. Edvard Munch used an expressive pictorial language to bring out a child's spiritual distress and despair. Käthe Kollwitz drew attention in her pictures to the misery of working-class children in the cities.

In Worpswede, the simplicity, sullenness and lack of sharpness of peasant children and poor-house children were an appealing subject for Paula Modersohn-Becker. She observed them with great empathy and without imposing her own feelings and ideas. By adopting this inner attitude towards the child facing her, and by using the artistic resources of close-up depiction and reduction to the most important details of form and content, she created pictures in which the children have become witnesses to their own existence and to their being as they are. Thus these pictures touch upon a deep layer of experience in the onlooker if he is able to face up to this experience. It was particularly in her paintings of children that she achieved what she was always aiming at when using the term "intimate": the unquestioning, kind-hearted closeness to the other person, who is left a free space for his own existence.

These depictions, which do not prettify their subject, tended and still tend to repel certain critics and observers of those times and ours.

In the painting Elsbeth in Garden Beside Glass Ball (c. 1902; Ill. XI), the little girl, with a child's unerring naturalness, is extending her little belly towards the onlooker, her hands behind her back. Her bonnet shining in the sunlight surrounds her round child's face. Strands of hair fall loosely on to her bright blue dress with its reddish shimmer. A large glass ball stands on a post behind and to the left of Elsbeth. The upper edge of the picture cuts through the ball. The house and garden of the Modersohn family are reflected in the ball. The outlines of the mirror image, transferred upwards, record the outlines of the genuine garden behind Elsbeth.

A green-brown harmony of colours prevails around the child. The round forms of glass ball, flower bed and bonnet are compositionally closely related to one another and to the square surface of the picture. They contrast with the post which, with its straight, angular massiveness, seems to lend the child support and safety.

The close formal interrelationship between the individual elements of the picture induces the onlooker to consider that the garden, and the glass ball with the house reflected in it, are attributes of Elsbeth. They are an indispensable part of this little person, and they mark off the area of her everyday life in house and garden.

Otto Modersohn approached this subject completely differently. The motifs in the painting Garden with Glass Ball and Elsbeth dating from 1903 (Ill. X) are almost the same as in the painting by his wife, except that Elsbeth is significantly also given a putto and a butterfly.

Otto Modersohn's style of painting is also very relaxed and summary. But while Paula deliberately avoided any anecdotal reference points which might be related to the passing of time, Otto Modersohn painted a delicate and sympathetic little picture showing a single cheerful moment experienced during a walk in the garden.

The Portrait of a Sick Girl from 1901 (Ill. XIII) shows the child looking at the onlooker from close up and a little way above. The softly melting facial features are fashioned in pale colours. Colourless light touches the forehead, nose and cheeks from above. The pouting lips and the neck are shown darkly and in shadow. A strand of hair detaching itself from the lustreless blonde hair delicately frames the left ear. The white-grey-beige surface of the sky yields a dark outline around the head. The dress, with its dark green and its greyish blue worked over with beige, makes a lifeless impression. The tree, with its animated dabbings of paint, forms an intentional contrast to the quietness of the girl, but with its white blossoms and dark green leaves it also makes a lifeless impression—the cardboard and a sienna-coloured paint layer are seen shining through.

The onlooker's attention is continually seized by the girl's facial features: the mouth makes a dumb impression, and the eyes have a weak look; they seem to have departed on a journey inwards.

The portrait of the GIRL IN FRONT OF WINDOW from 1902/1903 (Ill. XII) is constructed like a still life. The head before the window cross is clearly fashioned in three dimensions, using warm flesh tints which contrast with the cool hues of the surrounding surface which are in various degrees of brightness of the colours blue and green. A candlestick and a vase beside the girl are given gloss and volume by the light shining on them. They stand almost silhouette-like before the brighter background seen through the window. The window cross divides up the elements of the garden and landscape, forming them into an almost abstract, ornamental composition which is held together by a brightened surface through which the black slate on which the picture is painted can be seen. This composition is enlivened by finely incised plant motifs.

The dark red curtain on the right takes up the red of the girl's lips and lends the picture a warmer tone. A striking feature is the coltsfoot flowers behind the girl's head. They shine out like little suns from a remote darkness.

Paula Modersohn-Becker liked to assign garlands or individual blooms to the children in her paintings. She decorated herself with them in her later self-portraits. To her, this Jugendstil derived motif became the embodiment of a naive, childish joy of living.

In this picture too, the flowers are to be understood as relating directly to the girl. Their simplicity and warm luminous power relate—in a secret, possibly polar, way—to the child's condition. That condition finds expression in a slight inclination of the head, in the mouth and particularly in the eyes.

From summer 1902 onwards, remarks suggestive of marital tension appear in Paula and Otto Modersohn's diaries. In May 1902, a year after the wedding, Paula noted[109]: "I feel as if it would probably be difficult to continue one's life to the end in a good and great manner. The beginning, the part up to now, has been easy. Now it is likely to be harder, with some inner struggles involved. Casting the nets is what a lot of people do, but the point is that you then have to make a catch!" Paula only had a few years for her great work. In order to haul in the nets, she had to withdraw and follow her own law.

Despite being so generous and considerate, Otto Modersohn found it difficult always to accept Paula's need to work in seclusion. His annoyance at this was recorded in the diary as follows[110]: "I'm afraid Paula is very afflicted by these modern ideas. She's also something of an egoist. She brusquely and inconsiderately dismisses anyone she thinks isn't deep and subtle enough. [...] I've often had to put up with this brusque egoism myself. Are all talented women like this? Paula is very talented as an artist, and I'm amazed at her progress. If only more human virtues went with it. That must be the most difficult thing for a woman: to be highly spiritual and intelligent but still all a woman."

This and numerous other diary entries are sufficient proof that Otto Modersohn was the only person to recognize his wife's genius and was well able to sympathize with the sufferings of her "artistic solitude"[111]: "No one understands her. Her mother, brothers, sisters and aunts have all tacitly agreed that Paula won't achieve anything; they don't take her seriously. And the same applies in Worpswede—no one ever asks about her work. Vogeler says: 'To a woman, art has to be very unimportant'; he never asks about Paula, and he never comes to Brünjes' studio (Paula's workplace). He doesn't acknowledge

14
With Otto Modersohn and Elsbeth, 1902/03

or appreciate her, and regards her as completely unsuccessful. So be it. I am pleased at my Paula, who really is a great painter. Even today, she is painting better than Vogeler or Mackensen. Despite what her family thinks, my assessment of her is not dictated by my love towards her. She will go on striving and growing in solitude and will astonish everyone one day. I'm looking forward to that."[112]

By the end of 1902, Paula Modersohn-Becker seems to have climbed to a new stage. She made a notable entry in her diary when under the influence of works by the painter Mantegna[113]: "He has an tremendous three-dimensionality which gives a great essential strength. That's exactly what's missing from my work. [. . .] My second main difficulty is my lack of intimacy. The way that Mackensen interprets the people here isn't grand enough for me; it's too much in the genre style. If anyone were able, he would have to write them down in runic characters."

The word "Runenschrift" ("runic characters") is a key word in Paula Modersohn-Becker's art. What she meant by it will be inferred from her later pictures.

In these winter months of 1902/1903, while she was gaining a clearer view of her artistic goal, she became aware that something new was making itself felt in the development of her personality: "It's strange: I feel as if my voice had gained some completely new sounds and as if my whole being had acquired new possibilities. I feel it growing larger and wider within me. God grant that something may become of me."[114]

It seems logical that a trip to Paris was now due. The rural, idyllic surroundings of Worspwede could not impart to her what she needed now: stimulation and the possibility of conflicting with the great world outside. So she went to Paris again in 1903.

"Life, the curly thing within itself"

Paris and Worpswede, 1903–1905

Paula Modersohn-Becker needed a few days to feel that she was in the right place, but she then soon felt that this stay in Paris would also be fruitful to her. She once again worked in the Cola Rossi academy, and continued her studies in museums and galleries.

She acquired some valuable ideas through the two Rilkes, who were also in Paris. She was oppressed by the joyless relationship between the couple: "If only they were a bit more cheerful. Now they are moping, and doing it twice over," she wrote to her husband.[115] Clara worked in the studio of Rodin the sculptor. To Paula's way of thinking, Clara "exaggerated too much" and talked only of herself and her work.[116] The poet was suffering a deep crisis in his work at that time. He arranged for Paula Modersohn-Becker to have the opportunity of meeting Rodin. It is notable that Rilke, in his letter of recommendation, did not describe Paula as a painter, but as the "femme d'un peintre très distingué". Thus she concealed her painting from him too. If he did not mention her painting in his Worpswede monograph, this was simply because he did not know her works at that time. He did not see them until he came to Worpswede in Christmas 1905.

The aspect of Rodin that most impressed Paula Modersohn-Becker was his drawings. But the impression they made did not manifest itself in her own drawings and sketches. Instead, she set about studying the art of the past with still greater intensity. She systematically went to the Louvre and produced numerous drawn copies of sculptures and paintings. In doing this she was not interested in learning the history of art or in building up a reserve of forms to use. "Rather, her drawn copies are a constant attempt to use old works in order to find her way to simple, compact forms and, through the work of drawing, to convert these visual experiences into her own ideas regarding form."[117]

During her stay in Paris in 1900, she had studied almost nothing but predella panels from the early Italian Renaissance period. Here, she was interested in early attempts at reproducing space with the aid of central perspective, which had just been discovered. Thus she never reproduced details of the contents, or details which were especially appealing in terms of aesthetics; instead, she only reproduced the compositional framework of such a panel, as for example in the drawn copy, made in 1900, of the scene depicting the burial of St. Bernard in a painting from the school of Giotto (Ill. 17, 18).

During her later stays in Paris in 1903 and 1905, Paula Modersohn-Becker had the same intention in mind when studing Greek frieze reliefs and medieval tomb and architectural sculpture.

16
Lucas Cranach the elder
VENUS IN LANDSCAPE
16th century
Wood, 38 x 25 cm
Paris, Louvre

15
VENUS, copied from Lucas Cranach (Louvre)
1903–1906
Charcoal, 15.5 x 24 cm
Bunzlau sketch-book with drawn copies

Her manner of selecting originals to copy from, with a view to developing her own style for human figures, is clearly seen in her copies of full-length paintings and sculptures. The omission of all details, the emphasis on outline, the slight modelling in the internal hatching, and finally the preference for simple walking and standing motifs—these peculiarities of her drawing style are also to be found in her drawings from the nude (Ill. 15, 16).[118]

A decisive feature of her artistic development in these weeks was her encounter with ancient Japanese and Egyptian art (see Ill. 19, 20), as well as classical Greek art. The preparation for these stirring experiences had taken place in Worpswede.

After going to an exhibition of ancient Japanese art, she wrote in her diary[119]: "I was seized by the great strangeness of these things. Our own art seems to me

17
Giotto school
BURIAL OF ST. BERNARD
14th century
Paris, Louvre

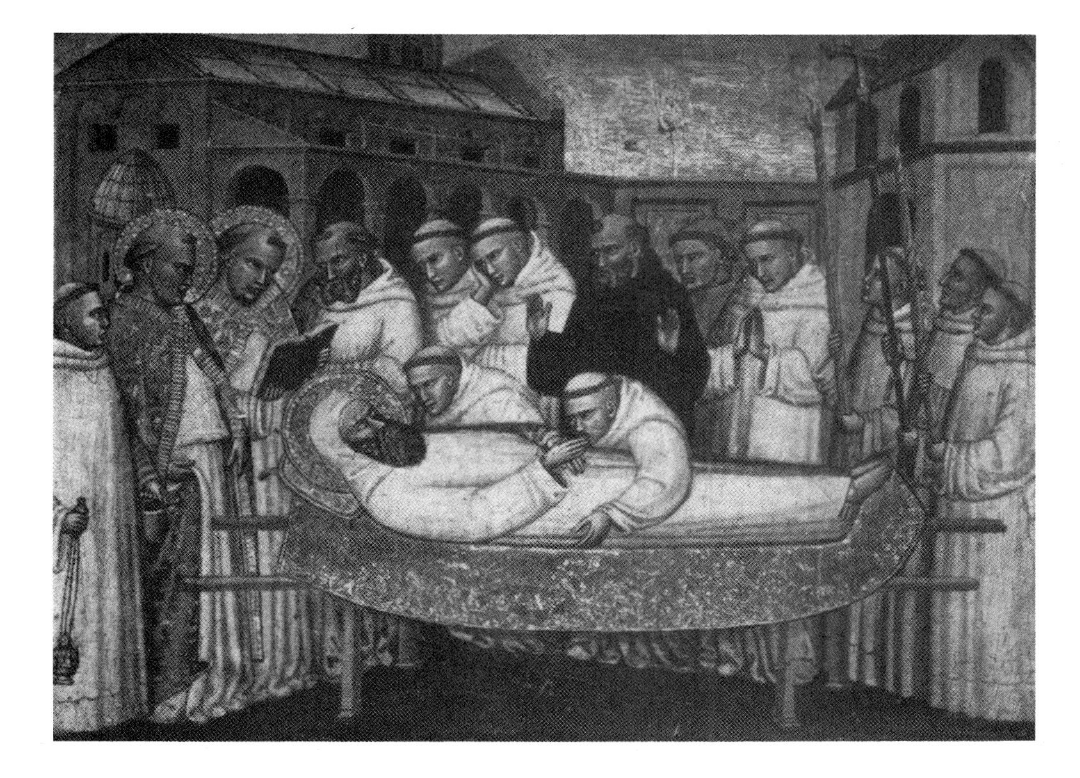

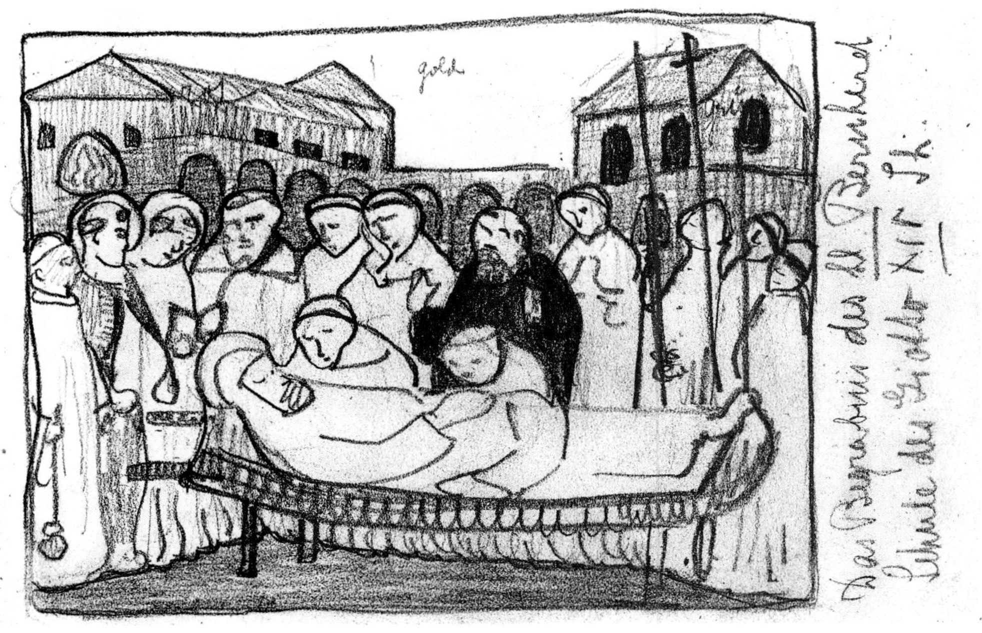

18
BURIAL OF ST. BERNARD
1900
Pencil and charcoal, 15.5 x 24 cm
Bunzlau sketch-book with drawn copies

to be much too conventional. It is very inadequate at expressing the feelings which pass through our inner being. This problem seems to me to be better solved in ancient Japanese art. Nocturnal scenes, and things which are gruesome, delightful, feminine or coquettish—all this seems to me to be expressed in a more childish and apt way than anything we would do. The chief emphasis must be placed on the main points!!" And in a letter to Otto Modersohn: "In this way one feels how these people related to nature."[120] She thought she was able to look at people in a quite different way after this visit to the exhibition.

Ever since the 1860s, avant-garde painters in France had taken great interest in ancient Japanese art. In a phase of European painting characterized by endeavours to overcome the illusion of depth, ancient Japanese art provided a stimulus because it was an art form which had, long before, achieved the two-dimensionality desired. It was particularly in the works of Gauguin, van Gogh and

20
Egyptian Lion Recumbent
Paris, Louvre

19
Egyptian Lion Recumbent (Louvre)
1903–1906
Pencil and charcoal, 15.5 x 24 cm
Bunzlau sketch-book with drawn copies

the Nabis that Paula Modersohn-Becker had herself seen the effects of that art form.

It was in the art of classical antiquity that she found the "greatest simplicity" she had always been looking for: "Until now I have regarded classical art as something very alien. I thought it beautiful in itself, but I could not find any connection between it and modern art. But now I have found the connection and I believe that this as a step forward. I feel that there is an inner relationship between classical art, especially early classical art, and Gothic art, and also between Gothic art and my sense of form. This great simplicity of form is a wonderful thing. I always endeavoured to lend the simplicity of nature to the heads I painted or drew. Now I have a deep feeling of how I can learn by looking at classical heads. How great and simple is the manner in which they are conceived! Forehead, eyes, mouth, nose, cheeks, chin—that is all. It sounds so simple but it is in fact a great, great deal."[121]

By her new way of seeing, she obtained a new idea of the whole of French art in her visits to the Louvre: "[...] this creation on the basis of the present moment"[122] was an important realization to her. "This way of not putting the finishing touches to a work is something much practised by the French. The flexibility of their nature helps them here. We Germans always dutifully paint our pictures all the way through, and we are too ponderous to produce a small coloured sketch extempore, although such a sketch often has more to say than a finished painting."[123]

She was repeatedly attracted by Rembrandt's works. Ever since her stay in Berlin, but now to a greater extent, she found in his paintings the thing she was herself attempting to express: "Life, the curly thing within itself."[124] Or the "soft vibration" and the "strangely waiting thing hovering above dull objects (skin, Otto's forehead, fabrics, flowers): that is the feature whose great, simple beauty I must strive to achieve"[125]. Later on she wanted to "show the rushing, full, exciting features within the colours, the mighty power of the colours"[126].

These concepts, which essentially circle around the same topic, re-appear repeatedly in the evidence she gave concerning herself during her weeks in Paris. Like the term "Runenschrift" ("runic characters"), they are a key to the deeper understanding of her work. Paula Modersohn-Becker seems to dive repeatedly into those layers where the contrariety of things merges into a single unity; where the current of life can be heard in profound quietude, in a timeless and spaceless realm. The following two passages from letters clearly point in this direction:

"And then there are hours in which existence and non-existence flow into one another as in our old garden. You don't notice much of this. They are concealed, delicate, evanescent things which shun the eye of the sun, but such are the things of which my life consists. Compared with these things, everything else looks ridiculously small: I mean all the external events that confront me and signify happiness and unhappiness to many people. Those are the things, the hours, that constitute my art, my life, my religion, my soul."[127]

"Oh, this depth in our heart. This depth was long veiled in mists and I had little knowledge and little idea of it. And now I feel as though each of my inner experiences was lifting these veils and I was looking into this sweet, trembling blackness which conceals within it everything that makes life worth while. I have a strong feeling that everything I have previously dreamt of regarding my own art had not been nearly sufficiently internalized when I experienced it. It must go through the whole person, through every fibre of our being."[128]

In view of this intensity and depth of experience, it is scarcely surprising that the painter, throughout her life, felt restlessly driven to turn this experience into art. Something comparable can be seen in the letters of Vincent van Gogh. Some decades later, Wassily Kandinsky put it in the following words: "Pure harmony comes to the fore. The soul arrives at an abstract vibration which is more complicated and transcendental."[129]

It was her longing for her husband and for Elsbeth that induced Paula Modersohn-Becker to return home earlier than planned. In early spring, Otto Modersohn confided the following to his diary: "After her return from Paris, my dear Paula brings me the most wonderful things: on the one hand, a deepening of our love, which is wonderful [...]. And then her art [...]."[130]

The artistic travelling baggage that Paula brought with her from Paris was manifold and rich. She gradually unpacked it in the pictures she produced in the following years.

After returning to Worpswede, Paula Modersohn-Becker immediately went back to work. "I have brought with me a great urge for the things of nature, an urge I obtained from Rodin, Cottet and Paris. That is probably the healthy aspect of my trip to Paris. Within me there burns a desire to grow great in simplicity," she wrote in her diary in April (BT 359). For Paula, her "quiet blissfulness," the "factor that makes me happy," lay in the "daily round" and not in "what is usually called one's experiences", she informed her aunt Marie Hill in England.[131] "My trip to Paris has passed me by without my now really thinking of it any more. I myself am often surprised at this. While I was there, it gave me new knowledge and now I am busy developing myself further on the basis of that knowledge. I think I am living a very intense life in present time." Her Parisian impressions had once again penetrated into those deep layers from which they produced their direct effect.

She produced some 150 pictures in the years between her two stays in Paris in 1903 and 1905. They include only a few landscapes pure and simple. But

Paula Modersohn-Becker continued to paint children and adults in natural surroundings. She also continued her series of scenes from Worpswede life. It was particularly in paintings with several human figures in natural surroundings that some of the knowledge gained in Paris was transformed into art: "When drawing amid natural surroundings, I then feel that I have to seek out many strange forms and overlaps. I like the feeling of things pushing themselves into and above one another. I only need to be careful when developing and refining this feeling," she wrote in her diary on 25 February 1903 (BT 345).

A person looking at the painting PERAMBULATOR WITH GOAT AND CHILDREN (1905; Ill. VIII) sees this little scene from a child's perspective. The picture is dominated by dark, earthy, brown hues. Reddish to orange surfaces, mainly in the children's faces, lend a warm harmony to the clayey impression. The trees extend far beyond the upper edge of the picture. With their trunks and branches, they cut strange forms out of the surface of the sky, a surface descending far down the painting. Looked at by themselves, these areas of sky, with their saturated brightness, are well to the front of the painting. This prevents any illusion of depth, even though the forms of the children, the perambulator and the goat overlap one another.

The cut-out areas of sky, and the trees, combine to produce a network of shapes and dark lines that is reminiscent of glass windows. Contrasting with this are the shapes of the children and of the perambulator, which are more graphically conceived. The way in which the surfaces, with their saturated brown and glowing red tones, "push themselves into and above one another" results in a composition in which there is hardly any objective representation. On the other hand, the bright forms of the goat and birch tree, painted with a slight three-dimensionality, are depicted with a more obvious realism.

The picture is painted with light brush-strokes. These lend the composition the character of something rushing and full, of something living, as the artist herself would have said. They underline the artistic unity, seen here, of colour and form, human figure and nature.

The period after her visit to Paris in 1903 gave this artist two new subjects for paintings: portraits of small children and depictions of motherhood. It is certain that in these paintings she expressed in artistic terms her longing to have a child of her own. She was not able to satisfy this longing in her loving relationship with little Elsbeth. As can be seen from the evidence she herself provides, this longing became ever stronger in 1903/4. But it would be a bad mistake to disparage her manner of dealing with this subject matter by describing it as a painted version of a "woman crying out for her child"[132]. Each of the paintings in question has an artistic value of its own, transcending the artist's personal situation.

For Paula Modersohn-Becker, motherhood had a religious dimension to it. In Christmas 1900 she wrote to her future husband[133]: "And then, you know, it is such a festival for women, because this motherhood lives on in every woman. It is all so holy. It is a mystery, and to me it is so deep and impenetrable and delicate and all-embracing. [...] Motherhood and death are my religion because I cannot comprehend them." As a woman, she shared in the mystery of birth and life.

Otto Modersohn did not think that his wife was properly made for motherhood. "My idea was always that her life should be entirely dedicated to her great art," he wrote to Gustav Pauli in 1919[134)]. This attitude bespeaks the expe-

XVII
Still Life With Clay Jug, Peonies and Oranges
1906
Oil on canvas, 61 x 49.5 cm
Privately owned

XVIII
Still Life With Jug
1903
Distemper on cardboard, 51.5 x 49.5 cm
Bremen, Kunsthalle

XIX
Still Life With Bunch of Dahlias
1907
Oil on canvas, 46 x 55 cm
Privately owned

XX
Portrait of Rainer Maria Rilke
1906
Oil distemper on cardboard, 32.3 x 25.4 cm
Bremen, Ludwig Roselius Collection

XXI
Sisters
1906
Oil distemper on cardboard, 58.5 x 40 cm
Privately owned

XXII
Mother Lying With Child
1906
Oil distemper on canvas, 82 x 124.7 cm
Bremen, Ludwig Roselius Collection

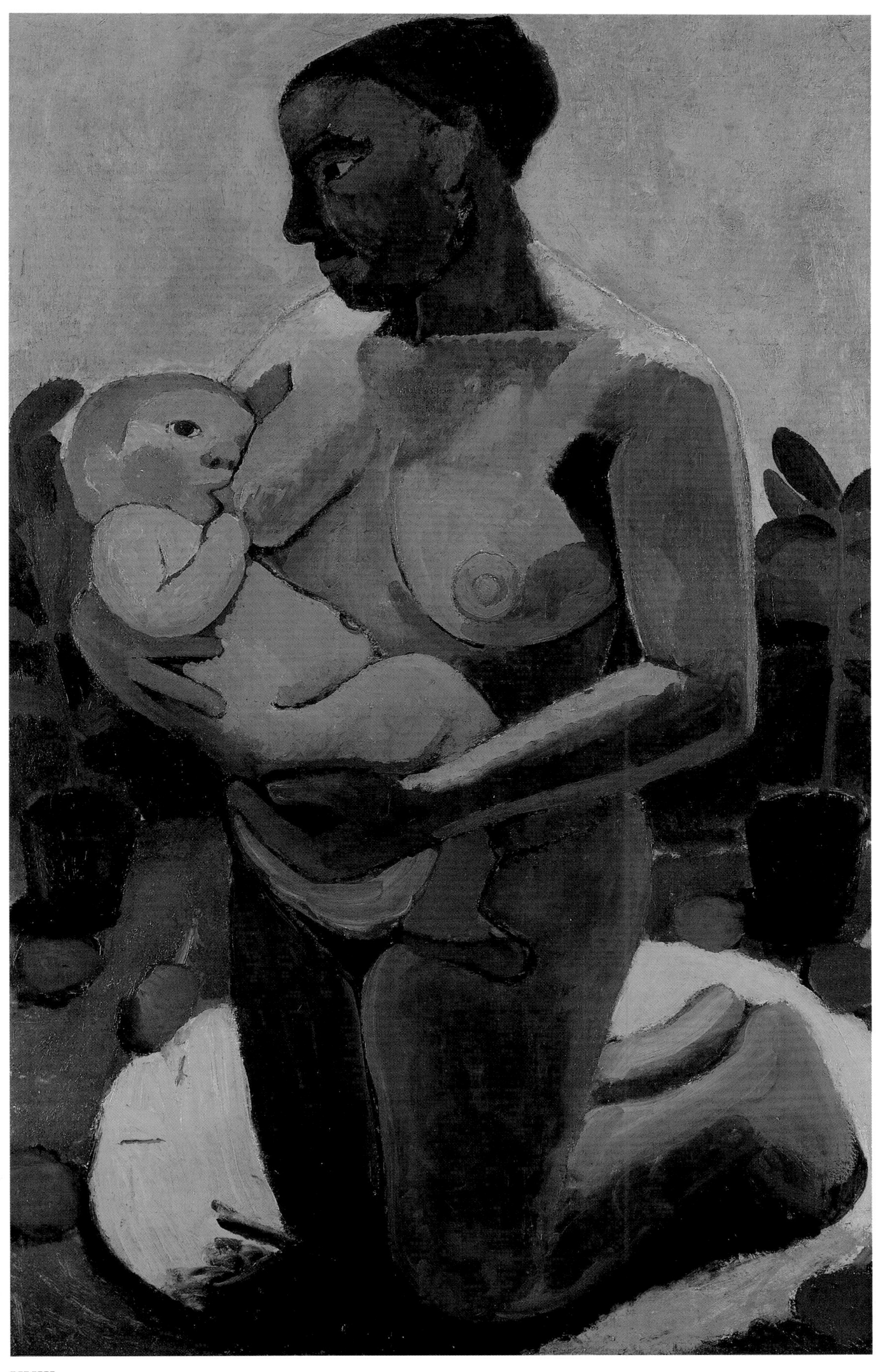

XXIII
MOTHER KNEELING WITH CHILD
1907
Oil on canvas, 113 x 74 cm
Berlin, Staatliche Museen Preussischer Kulturbesitz Berlin, Nationalgalerie

XXIV
Portrait of Lee Hoetger
1906
Paper on cardboard
Bremen, Ludwig Roselius Collection

rience of a husband who had often had the painful experience of seeing his wife's needs and wished to avoid further ordeals.

Paula Modersohn-Becker depicted the subject of mother and child again and again, in a new way every time. In the end, she found ways of expressing herself which pointed far beyond her generation as regards the maturity of their artistic design and the overall binding force of the statement they made.

In the picture SLEEPING CHILD (c. 1907; Ill. XV), the cradle is seen from above. The child slumbers, softly bedded in the cushions.

The warm red of the dress is absorbed in the checkered pattern of the cushion, whose soft three-dimensionality is fashioned with various gradations. The bed sheet also follows this pattern. The beige and brown tones darken in shade towards the foot of the bed. The dark-brown surfaces of the cradle create a kind of frame within which the cradle becomes the embodiment of a safe and peaceful space.

The painting MOTHER SUCKLING HER CHILD (c. 1903; Ill. XIV) appeals to the onlooker in a peculiarly direct and even suggestive way.

Bright and warm forms come forth from a nameless, spaceless darkness. These are the physical shapes of mother and child, which seem to have been driven from within so as to form firm round shapes. The woman's heavy left hand holds the baby. The child rests on her lap, supported on a broad basis. His hair is stuck to his hot little head, his legs are pulled up into a baby's position and crossed over. His eyes are closed and he is entirely given over to drinking. He does not see or feel the coarseness of his mother's dark hands, accustomed to hard work.

The child's plump little hand lies trustingly in the woman's right hand, just at the level of her breast. This is the centre of the picture, and is also where the onlooker's line of vision meets the picture. The area of the breast free of the jacket is in the shape of an inverted heart. The nourishing breast bulges forth like a heavy drop from the upper tip of the "heart".

The woman's head is looked at from below, and the upper edge of the picture cuts through it. Her eyes, with an indescribable heaviness, are looking out beyond the child. They attract the onlooker's gaze and take him out of the picture. Then the bright centre in the area of the woman's breast and heart once again catch the onlooker's eye, afterwards taking him to the baby and then upwards to where the buttoned-up jacket, almost painfully, prevents the ends of breast area and neck area from coming into contact with one another.

In this picture, Paula Modersohn-Becker depicts firstly the relationship between mother and child, and secondly the suckling process, in a way that cannot be described by the usual terms such as "mother's love" or "intimacy". The core of the statement being made affects the onlooker directly, using the untranslatable language of artistic technique.

Otto Modersohn was not always able to approve unconditionally of his wife's artistic development. This can be seen from one of his diary entries which has in the past been incompletely quoted more than once, and has therefore become "the crystallized core of the legend of a wife who is not understood by her husband"[135]. The full diary entry runs as follows: "At the Meyers' house, I saw some works by Rheylaender and Paula. Rheylaender's were very unpleasant, superficial, conventional—a superficial story tossed down on paper. This is a dangerous approach, which does not lead to further development. There are lots of people like that at the academy. Paula is just the opposite. She hates conventional things and is now making the mistake of preferring to do everything in an angular, ugly, bizarre, wooden way. The colour is fabulous, but what about the form and the manner of expression? Hands like spoons, noses like pistons, mouths like wounds, expressions like cretins. She gives herself too much to do. Two heads, four hands on a very small surface: that is the minumum she works with, and she puts in children as well. As usual, it is difficult to give her any advice."

In the second part of this entry, Otto Modersohn wonders whether the depiction of ugliness in some of Paula's paintings does not go a little far. Integrating ugliness into art was something quite new at the beginning of the century. Otto Modersohn was possibly afraid that Paula was "being enticed into a dead end by the fashions of the day"[136].

However, the first few sentences of this quotation show once again how highly he rated his wife's skill. This also applies to the period when the two of them, more and more, were developing in different directions artistically.

1904, the next year, passed without any major occurrences. Some short trips interrupted the uniformity of everyday life. It can be seen from Paula's letters that she withdrew more and more and enjoyed being alone for several days. Then she retired to her studio at the Brünjes' house and played at being "Paula Becker". She wrote to her husband: "Do you know that you're in the background of my freedom? That's what makes that freedom so nice. If I were free and didn't have you, it would of no value to me"[137]. In a letter written the same day, her sister Milly was told the following[138]: "It's so strange: I am pleased almost every time Otto and I are not together. We have the strange pleasure of looking at each other mentally from afar, and then we can look forward to seeing one other again and can write to one other. I can also now do certain things which would remain undone if Otto were there. Thus I ordered cold rice and cold apple compote for us this lunchtime." Otto Modersohn understood her needs, but sometimes suffered greatly from them.

The winter and a "bad period of work" depressed Paula. Finally, in February 1905, Otto Modersohn once again agreed to a trip to Paris.

21
Otto Modersohn
PAULA WEARING HER CHAPEAU GRIS IN PARIS, 1905
Charcoal, 17.8 x 24.5 cm
Fischerhude, Otto Modersohn foundation museum

"The thing in itself—in the right mood"

Paris, 1905

On 14 February 1905, Paula Modersohn-Becker went to her beloved Paris once again, while her mother looked after her husband and the child. She expressed her unrestrained joy in a poem she wrote in a postcard to her husband (BT 393):

"... à Paris
freu ich mich wie noch nie. [I am more pleased than ever before.]
Je suis la tienne
Ta petite parisienne
Avec son chapeau rond
Elle va voir le monde
Avec un chapeau gris
Sans soucis."

As usual, she needed a little time to be able to enjoy Paris properly. But then she hurled herself with real hunger into the bustle of the carnival season, which included a little flirt. These weeks were enhanced because she spent much time with her sister Herma who was preparing for her French studies by working as an au pair in Paris.

At the beginning of this stay in Paris, Paula Modersohn-Becker registered herself for a course in painting nudes at the Julian academy. She wrote to Worspwede of a typical episode from her work at the academy[139]: "They look at my paintings very suspiciously, and when there is a break and I have gone away from my easel, six of them come and stand in front of it, debating my work. A Russian woman asked me whether I really see things the way I paint them, and who taught me this. Then I told a lie and proudly said: 'Mon mari'. Then she thought the truth had dawned on her and said with relief: 'Oh, you paint like your husband does.' They do not suspect that I paint as I myself paint."

As always, she went to museums and exhibitions, busily making sketches. This time she was attracted not so much by the old masters as by the most modern painters of all. She went and saw Vuillard and Denis, the Nabis, in their studio. She very much liked Maillol's small human figures. "Retrospective exhibitions of van Gogh and Seurat, from which I do not learn any more than I knew before"; and in the Fauves I "cannot properly tell where there's a screw loose, but I have a vague feeling that there's one missing somewhere"[140]. The really inspiring "thunderstorm" was probably Gauguin, but we can only tell this from her own paintings, the still lifes from the following period.

In the middle of these "rich, wonderful" weeks came the news of the death of Otto Modersohn's mother. Paula had not known her closely and felt so good in Paris that she was glad to accept her husband's suggestion that she need not come to the funeral but could stay in Paris. She even managed to persuade her husband to make the trip to Paris.

Although Paula had been very much looking forward to seeing him again, no really joyous companionship arose. "He was very jealous of Paris, of French art, French ease, Boulevard Miche Boulgaren etc. He got the idea that I would prefer to stay in Paris and thought nothing of Worpswede. Well, you know him, don't you?"[141]

But from Otto Modersohn's point of view these weeks were different. He was still greatly affected by his mother's illness and death. He later wrote in a letter that it had, for him, been "nothing more than a series of misunderstandings"[142].

Paula Modersohn-Becker brought back with her from her third stay in Paris an increased interest in still life. Some seventy paintings of this type are known today, fifty of which were produced between 1905 and 1907. The subjects she chose for these paintings were simple objects from her domestic and living surroundings, objects which she lovingly collected and to which intimate memories were attached: jugs, vases, plates, chains, ribbons and, again and again, flowers and fruit. It was in these still lifes that she was able to pursue in the most direct fashion her artistic goal of monumentalizing forms by simplifying them and giving them colour[143]. "The great style of the form requires a great style in the colour," she noted on a piece of paper in May 1906 (BT 445).

It is in the still lifes that her artistic concern with contemporary painters is at its most obvious. It was from Cézanne that she derived the idea that the space depicted should be severely constructed and that the arrangement of the picture surface should be well balanced[144], and Gauguin gave her some pointers on how to make the colours independent[145]. These were impulses along her own particular artistic path, a path she had pursued even in her early paintings, particularly the landscapes.

Along with those of Cézanne, her still lifes "are the most important contribution to this type of painting produced around the turn of the century"[146].

The same jug with a handle, glazed in yellow, appears on the three still lifes depicted here. Paula Modersohn-Becker probably acquired it in Paris in 1905.[147] This artist's way of dealing with objective realism, with colour and form, and with the space and area of the picture, can all be seen from this jug.

The Still Life With Jug (1903; Ill. XVIII) looks positively like an old master in its mode of painting, its structure and its faithful reproduction of the objects. Like several of her still lifes, it is reminiscent of works by the painter Jean Baptiste S. Chardin, whom Paula knew but only once mentioned in passing.[148]

The onlooker looks diagonally down on to a surface on which a piece of white French bread, fruit and three vessels are loosely distributed. The warm coloured harmonies of these objects contrast with the cooler hues of the table and background surfaces.

The combination of objects is finely balanced in its colour and volume, and the manner of painting is compact throughout. This makes the picture appear quiet, and also gives a clear structure to the illusion of depth created. Only when the picture is examined in more detail does the spatial structure appear

22
Elsbeth With Doll on Amrum
1903
Charcoal, 17 x 10.5 cm
Inscribed: Elsbeth, Amrum
Paula Modersohn-Becker foundation

23
Hooded Child With Dog
c. 1906
Charcoal, 26 x 31.6 cm
Privately owned

24
Picture postcard dated 26.7.1903 to Paula's mother
Pencil, 9.3 x 14.1 cm
Inscribed: "Die drei Wattenläufer ("Three Walkers in the Mudflats")

unstable: there is a play, rich in tension, between the three-dimensionality, the area and the varying perspectives.

The surface on which the objects stand, and the background surface, are shown as two surfaces parallel to one another in the picture. The illusion of depth is created only by the physicality of the objects and by the spatial relationship between them. Delicate colour nuances, highlights and soft shadows allow the objects to unfold their sturdy three-dimensional structure. At the same time the oranges are showing a tendency to roll forwards out of the picture. The bread is looked at almost from above, strengthening the impression that the surface it stands on is tipping up. The left end of the left handle, and the cork of the bottle, are also seen from a raised perspective.

The arrangement of the objects within the surface of the picture makes a random impression. But it has been deliberately staged in this way: rhythmical lines direct the onlooker's gaze across the picture's surface, and thus again and again into the impression of space, which has to be repeatedly re-defined. The jug is the main actor in this play. Thanks to the large highlight at the point of its maximum expansion, which coincides with the centre of the picture, it directly attracts the onlooker's attention. The bread and the two oranges mark out the area for the jug by pushing the impression of space forwards beyond the area of the picture, and by guiding the onlooker's gaze around the jug: the bread moves into an indeterminate darkness on the very left, and the oranges go to the right, where another line, which includes an orange, a lemon and a small bowl, leads up to the brown bottle. The slenderness of the bottle gives the jug an even more bulging appearance. At the same time it gives an illusion of space behind the jug.

The colours of the objects are part of this mobile game being played with the illusion of space. The colours are gradated according to intensity and warmth, so that the luminous strength of the oranges and bread makes them urge their way forwards, while the bottle, with its unobtrusive brown, remains in the background. The jug, which stands in the middle between the front and rear, is also given a middling amount of colour intensity.

The objects in this picture play a peculiar dual rôle. The jug and bottle are conceived of as objects whose colours serve the purposes of objective realism. On the other hand, the colours of the flowers, fruit and bread make them strive for independence. This gives the oranges, in particular, a peculiar ambivalence: on the one hand they are conceived of as objects with a realistic, tangible surface, but on the other hand they are seen as pure spherical objects with their own colours which create their own effect.

Paula Modersohn-Becker's STILL LIFE WITH CLAY JUG, PEONIES AND ORANGES (1906; Ill. XVII) touches upon the borders of the abstract. The game played with surface and with the illusion of space is taken to the extreme, so that the painting makes an almost surreal impression.[149] A few objects are reduced to very simple surfaces with few colours. The two-dimensionality is emphasized by black outlines and a painted structure determined by strong parallel brushstrokes. The black lines which symmetrically articulate the surface on which the objects stand resemble vanishing lines, and thus suggest a space which is given a still greater appearance of depth by a second jug, which is tiny in comparison with the main jug. Of the objects, the jug with the handles is the only one to have a flat kind of three-dimensionality. The peonies, on the other hand, have a fuller appearance, due to the relaxed manner in which they are painted. They are urging their way to the very front plane of the picture, the picture's surface, from which the black lines once again lead into the depths of the picture. But these depths are soon "tipped up" again and become a surface.

In contrast to the previously described still life, the objects are no longer depicted realistically as in a faithful reproduction of nature. They are converted into surfaces which have an independent colourfulness that lives from its own inner being. Only the large jug and the peonies have a certain realistic heaviness, but they are still not reproductions of real objects.

In the last few months of her life, Paula Modersohn-Becker painted still lifes in which she attained that beauty which—as she herself writes—results from the strength "with which an object is recorded"[150]. One of these is the STILL LIFE WITH BUNCH OF DAHLIAS dating from 1907 (Ill. XIX).

In this picture the objects have moved close up to the onlooker, and they therefore make a more direct impression than in the first still life. They are underpinned by a background built up of large surfaces which are outlined in black and run in parallel with the picture. The close interdependence between the objects and the surface of the picture is underlined by their dense painted structure, which is built up from broad brush-strokes. The impression of space arises only from the line, resembling a vanishing line, on the left of the vase, from the carefully thought-out gradations of brightness and warmth in the colours, and in particular from the objects themselves.

The jug with its handles, and the bunch of dahlias, have little three-dimensionality in themselves. Black outlines tie them into the basic two-dimensionality of the composition. The jug is seen almost frontally. With its two handles it looks almost ornamental. But the basket-like vase, like the ceramic plate, is seen diagonally and from above. The bright decoration on its dark brown belly, its bright lower edge, and the handle which runs diagonally towards the rear—all these lend it a certain three-dimensionality, but this is largely neutralized by the dahlias which are outlined in black and are located on the same plane as the surface of the picture.

This time, the main performer in the structure of the picture is the ceramic plate, which is the element in the picture really giving it an illusion of space. Clear and tangible in its shape and colour, it develops—without though being a reproduction of reality—the three-dimensional force of which Paula Modersohn-Becker said that "strength" becomes "beauty". It derives its warmly luminous colours from a paint substance which seems to have soaked up the sunlight and converted it into matter.

As if by accident, the plate is turned in such a way that the onlooker turns his head almost instinctively so to be able to recognize the bird motif clearly. In this way this motif becomes the secret driving force behind the movement of the onlooker's gaze when he is regarding the picture. The bird motif states where the movement of the onlooker's eye enters the picture and which direction it takes. Starting from the motif, one becomes aware of the gleaming red surface of a cloth (?) which pushes itself into the picture at the right lower edge. One's gaze is then moved diagonally upwards to the left, to the place where the plate touches the belly of the vase of dahlias. The handle of the vase then draws the onlooker's gaze upwards from the darkness of the vase to the dahlias which, like parts of a glass window, gleam before a cool, dark-grey surface. The left handle of the jug takes the movement of the gaze softly upwards and to the right. The coolly luminous turquoise green now seems to push the jug, which has a warm ochre tone, towards the front of the picture. The jug would in turn like to pass this pushing movement on to the ceramic plate and thrust it forwards and out of the picture, except that there is a patch of red in the corner, anchoring the plate to the surface of the painting.

The pictorial techniques, living in tense contrast with one another, are made to coincide with one another in this painting and serve the cause of the movement which takes place within the picture and by means of the picture. This phenomenon was observed in the landscapes described above (p. 57 f.). Stelzer[151] refers to it as "Wiederkehr" ("return") and notes on the subject: "It has become pointless to ask about centre of vision, vanishing lines, and horizon of vision. Scientific perspective, which can make plausible only a movement into the depth, but not the "return" from that depth, will not in future be able to continue the alluring rôle it has played in painting. It is not yet finished in van Gogh, it is hardly finished in Gauguin, but it is finished in Cézanne and Paula Modersohn-Becker." The "return" points to a further dimension of modernity in Paula Modersohn-Becker's works.

The onlooker is repeatedly turned back again on his way through the picture. He must retract his personal associations with the idea of space, and must associate himself objectively with the picture in order to come close to it. The traditional division between picture and onlooker is eliminated, and the onlooker is included in the process of producing the picture. He finally becomes aware of this process and thus experiences a transformation and an expansion of his possession of reality. Similar processes also take place when one is looking at works by the painters Braque, Klee, Baumeister, Rothko and Hartung—to name but a few.[152]

Starting from the ceramic plate, Paula Modersohn-Becker's STILL LIFE WITH BUNCH OF DAHLIAS exhales a new sensual plenitude, a real presence, which derives its strength from itself. The objects speak for themselves in their quiet existence.

"The thing in itself—in the right mood" was one of the phrases with which Paula Modersohn-Becker formulated her artistic goal.[153]

"I am myself"

Worpswede, 1905–1906

After her last stay in Paris, Paula Modersohn-Becker found it difficult to fit into the secluded life of Worpswede. She did not really succeed in doing so. It is true that her letters still contain descriptions of everyday events in a language reminiscent of her former cheerfulness. But there are now also new, dark tones. However, these utterances are supported by a great inner security. In the "very depths of her being" she felt "a great longing for the world", which her husband could not share with her. "From time to time I have a great desire to experience something more. It's a little difficult to cope with being as terribly tied down as one is when one is married," she wrote to her mother.[154] Paula missed having a woman "who I can talk to about my interests," she confessed apologetically to her sister Herma.[155] A difficult winter was imminent.

Paula was almost thirty years old, and she had previously made up her mind to have achieved something in art by the time she reached that age. She repeatedly observed that, to her, painting was a "fine art, which is difficult to accomplish".[156]

At the same time she sensed something of a new "adulthood" which made her afraid and which "I identify with 'resignation'"[157]. In Paula Modersohn-Becker, the awakening and radical change which occur in people of about thirty found its expression in her need for greater independence. It is also possible that she felt, in her husband, the absence of an antagonist with whom she could come into conflict. Even before her marriage she had described him as good-natured, sentimental and naive.

On the one hand, Otto Modersohn was sensitive in perceiving his wife's needs and requirements. He was "touchingly kind" towards her. This was brought to light by a "basic discussion": "Our life has become too monotonous and bourgeois. Paula suffers a great deal from this."[158] Taking stock of the matter, he became aware of the wealth brought him by living with Paula, and he made up his mind as follows: "But my life must become richer, more active and more full of experience. I am following Paula in this. Her instincts are very good. [. . .] I intend to make joyous use of every opportunity, and Paula will thank me for it by loving me. I shall keep younger, and I shall derive nothing but advantage from it, both as a person and as an artist." So he made a serious effort to brighten up the monotony of autumn and winter in Worpswede by making short trips to Berlin and Dresden, and also by visiting Carl Hauptmann in Schreiberhau.

On the other hand, it is also continually apparent from his diary entries that he finds it difficult to follow his wife artistically: "I don't enjoy Paula's art nearly

XXV
Self-Portrait With White Bead Necklace
1906
Oil on cardboard, 41.5 x 26 cm
Münster, Westphalian State Museum of Art and Cultural History

XXVI
Old Poorhouse Woman
c. 1905
Oil on canvas, 126 x 95 cm
Wuppertal, Von der Heydt Museum

XXVII
Old Poorhouse Woman With Glass Bottle
1907
Oil on canvas, 96 x 80.2 cm
Bremen, Ludwig Roselius Collection

XXVIII
FLOWER STILL LIFE WITH SUNFLOWER AND MALLOWS
1907
Oil on canvas, 90 x 65 cm
Bremen, Kunsthalle

XXIX
OLD PEASANT WOMAN
1907
Oil distemper on canvas, 75.5 x 57.7 cm
Detroit, Institute of Arts

XXX
Self-Portrait With Camellia Twig
1907
Oil distemper on cardboard, 62 x 30 cm
Essen, Museum Folkwang

XXXI
Self-Portrait With Two Flowers in My Raised Hand
1907
Oil on canvas, 55 x 25 cm
Privately owned

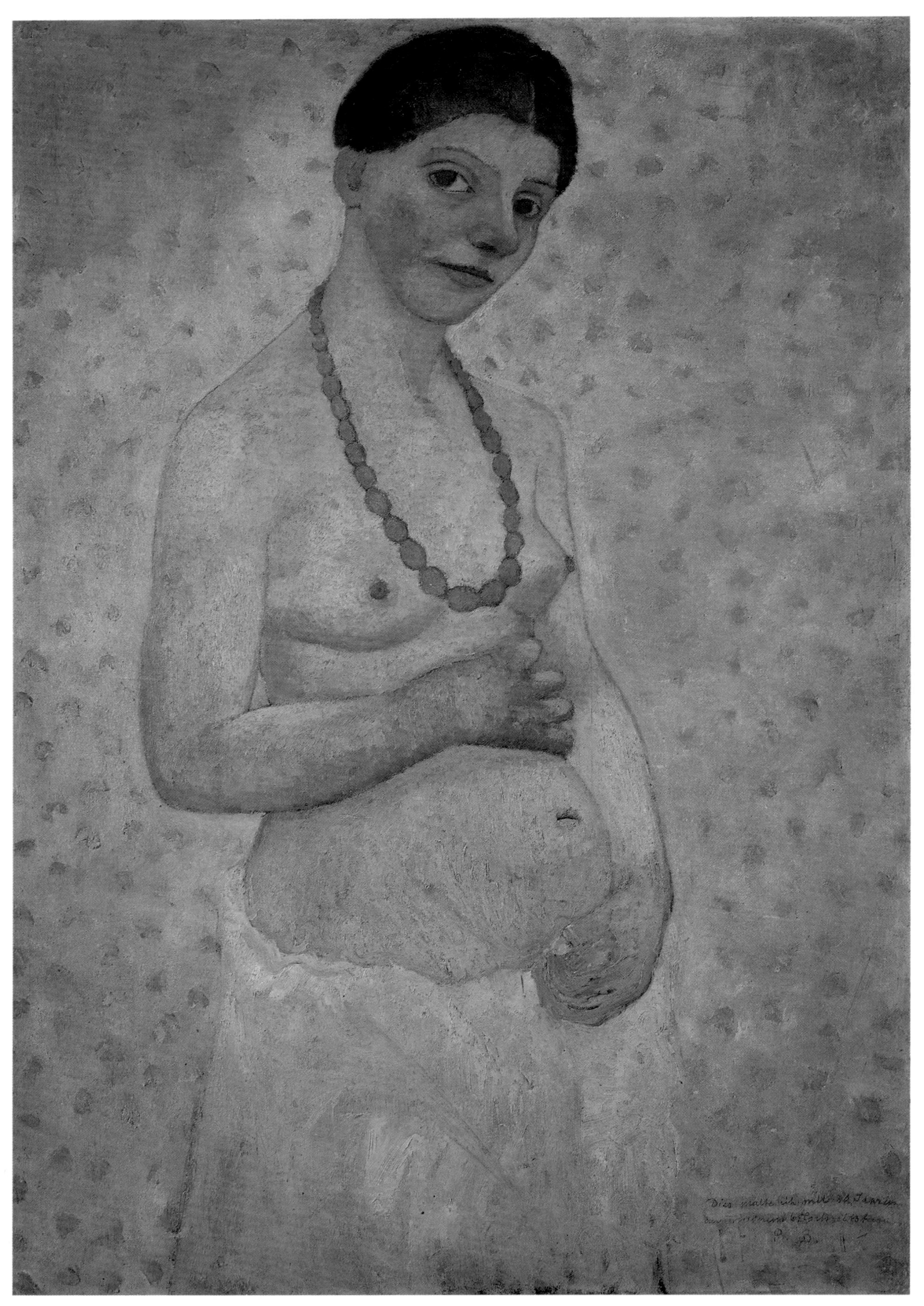

XXXII
Self-Portrait on My Sixth Wedding Anniversary
25 May 1906, inscribed at lower right:
"Dies malte ich mit 30 Jahren an meinem 6. Hochzeitstage. P. B."
("I painted this at the age of 30 on my 6th wedding anniversary. P. B.")
Oil distemper on cardboard, 101.5 x 70.2 cm
Bremen, Ludwig Roselius Collection

as much as I used to. She won't listen to advice—but that's very silly of her and a great pity. A tremendous waste of effort. Look at the things she could do! She paints life-sized nudes but she's no good at it, and she can't do life-sized heads either. [. . .] She's abandoning her magnificent studies. She does drawings as studies, so as to learn the technique, but that's all. She provides a great deal of colour—but she's too hard for a painter, particularly in her completed human figures. She reveres primitive paintings, which is a great pity for her—she ought to look at picturesque paintings. She wants to unite colour and form—but that can't be done the way she does it. She does not like to suppress the form, and that's a great mistake. She doesn't think enough about her art. She always keeps to the same ideas (?) when she works, and makes no further progress. It isn't easy for women to achieve anything decent."[159]

Such remarks on the work of Otto's wife ought perhaps not to be taken entirely literally. To some extent they appear to reflect the particular state of the marital relationship between the two artists. Otto Modersohn was himself in a depressive phase at that time. A little later, he sounds a completely different note in his diary: "I'm overjoyed, because I'm now certain that things are improving. [. . .] Paula has had a very favourable influence upon me. [. . .] The many pictures I painted in summer benefited me tremendously, and then there were the studies. At my side was Paula with her masterly still lifes and sketches. In their colours, they are the boldest and best things ever painted here in Worpswede."[160]

In the autumn weeks of that year, Paula again painted the well-known Worpswede motifs. They were large compositions this time. The two paintings PEASANT GIRL SITTING ON A CHAIR and GIRL PLAYING AN INSTRUMENT IN A BIRCH WOOD (both in the Roseliushaus in Bremen) are particularly impressive.

It was in those dismal weeks that the woman for whom Paula Modersohn had always longed came back to her: Clara Rilke-Westhoff was living in Worpswede again. The two women cautiously made contact with one another again. There is a description by Clara which throws light on Paula's state of mind at the time. The two of them were sitting by the stove of their studio on a winter afternoon. "Paula threw one piece of peat after another through the small twittering door into the fire, and one tear after another then rolled down her cheek, while she was explaining to me how very important it was for her to go out 'into the world' again, back to Paris. 'When I think of it like that, it is the world,' she said."[161]

The PORTRAIT OF CLARA RILKE-WESTHOFF (Ill. XVI), the first of a number of impressive portraits, dates from this period in late 1905.

The portrait is upright in format, and its few colours and its surfaces roughened up in "curly" style are executed liberally and with firmness.

The flesh tint of Clara's face and neck mediates between the darkness of the area around her head and the white of her dress. The red rose lends the picture a note of colour. The rose and the colour chosen for the dress evidently conceal references to Paula's and Clara's joint past: the white may be reminiscent of autumn 1900. At that time the two women, as "sisters in white", had come within the vision and under the influence of the poet Rainer Maria Rilke.

The rose is assigned to Clara as being the attribute of a female medieval saint. In the last few years of her artistry, Paula Modersohn-Becker developed her own many-sided symbolism which expresses itself in the gestures of the

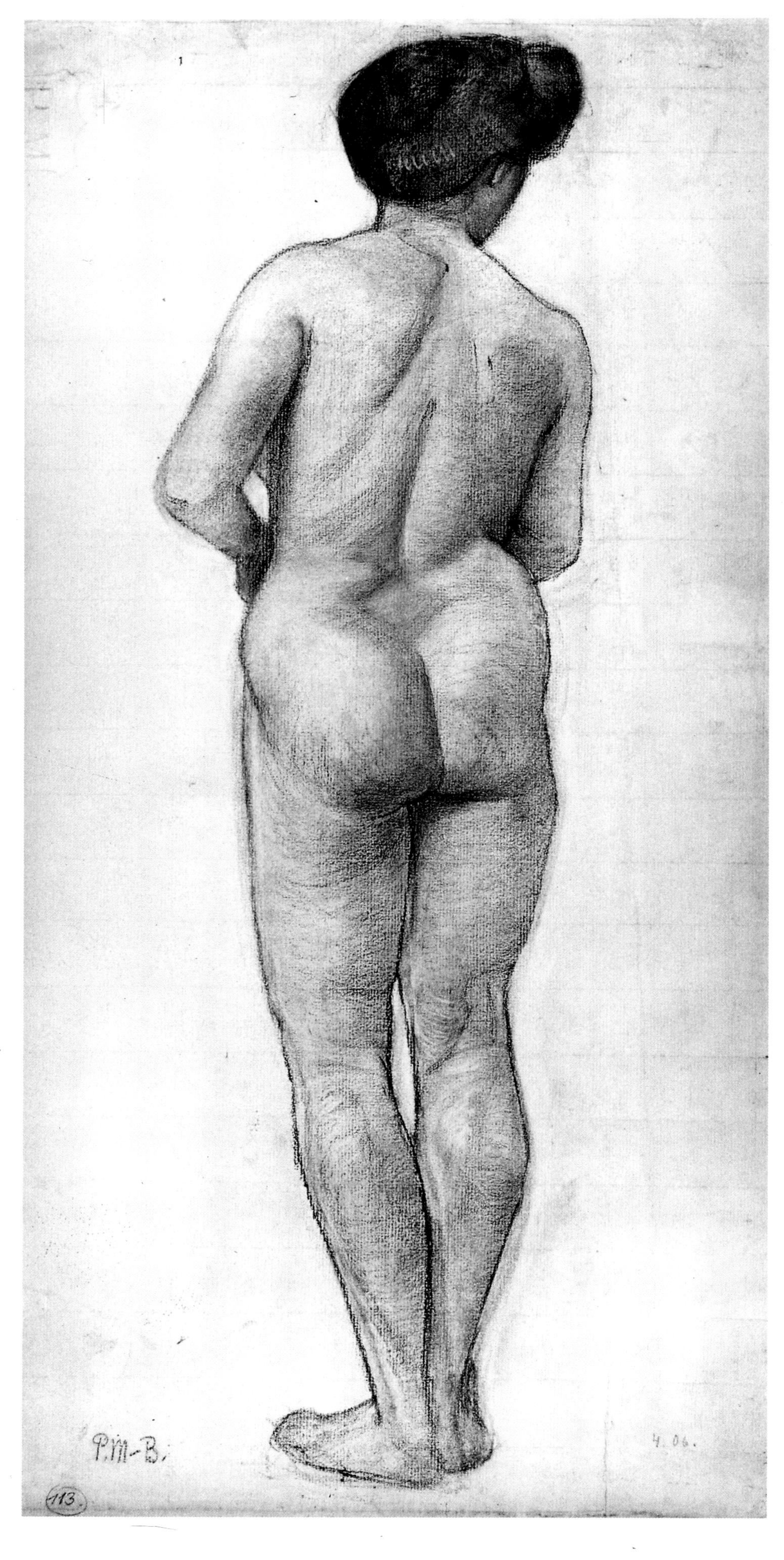

25
STANDING FEMALE NUDE
Rear view
1906
Charcoal, 65 x 31.3 cm
Signed at lower left: PMB
Dated at lower right: 4.06.

hands and in the objects added—usually chains, flowers or fruit. On the portrait of her friend Clara, the red rose can be understood as being a customary symbol of love and affection. In this meaning, the rose also refers to Clara's relationship with Rainer Maria Rilke. The rose played such a major rôle in his life and work that he eternalized it in poetry in his own epitaph.

The rose and the white dress are given a particular meaning by their association with the position of Clara's head and with her facial expression. Both of these are reminiscent of an unembarrassed and hopeful phase in her life, a phase lying far back in the past. The eyes which are edged in red and are looking far beyond the edge of the picture, and the downturned corners of the mouth, sum up the quintessence of years of married life: Clara Rilke-Westhoff's heavy features betray sadness and resignation, but at the same time they also express force and strength, possibly even defiance.

Rainer Maria Wilke came to Worpswede in late 1905 to see his wife and daughter. It was now that he first saw pictures by Paula Modersohn-Becker, and he immediately grasped their artistic significance. A letter he wrote to Karl von der Heydt expressed how they had affected him[162]: "The strangest thing was that Modersohn's wife was developing her painting in her entirely personal way, painting straight on regardless, depicting things which are very typical of Worpswede, but which no one has yet ever been able to see and paint. And in this very personal way of hers, her work was strangely related to Van Gogh and his artistic tendency."

The friendship between painter and poet was now renewed on another level. The two Rilkes gave Paula the understanding she so badly needed for her urge for more world and more art. Thus it was that, in the first weeks of the new year, she conceived her plan to move to Paris and to leave Worpswede, Otto Modersohn and Elsbeth, possibly for ever. Rilke even bought one of Paula's pictures. In the proceeds, which amounted to 50 marks, she naively saw the foundation for making her own living in the future.

Ever since her stay in Paris in February and March 1905, Paula Modersohn had written fewer and fewer letters, but their style was more determined. On her way to her great simplicity, she seemed to penetrate deeper and deeper into regions which are ruled by that silence which comes not before the word, but after it. Ottilie Reylaender-Böhme gives us an approximate picture of the change in Paula's appearance and being: "Her eyes became very quiet with the passing years, her face became even more spiritualized and beautiful, her movements lost their abruptness, and one sensed more of a gliding, swaying motion. [...] When in her presence, one was immediately below the surface and took part in matters which she could only produce by bringing them up from the depths; it was as if she had been collecting treasures of experience over a period of lifetimes, and these experiences were now gradually detaching themselves from the depths of her being. She spoke her sentences like magic formulae, as if consciously exercising a high office."[163]

The SELF-PORTRAIT WITH WHITE BEAD NECKLACE (Ill. XXV) was probably painted in the first few weeks of 1906.

The artist here depicts herself in warm brown, ochre and red hues. The delicate face is surrounded by a bright-blue and greyish-white surface which is its own source of light. A simple white necklace hangs round her neck, above the neck of the brown dress with its vermilion spots.

The round and oval surfaces and outlines of her hair, forehead, eyes, chin, necklace and neck correspond to and face towards one another. The slightly inclined axis of the body gives a rhythmical vibration to the play between those surfaces and outlines.

Paula Modersohn looks out of the picture from a little way below and to one side, as if from a tall narrow window. (In the original painting, the surrounding picture frame contributes considerably to this impression.) Her gaze, draped by her upper eyelids, looks past the onloooker. The impression she makes is rather shy and vulnerable, but still clear-headed and composed. But it is as if she needed the frame and the space behind the "window area" to protect her from what lies outside.

A letter to her mother, dated 19 January 1906 (BT 430 f.), shows how closely her artistic development was related to her way towards completeness as a human being. These moving lines were occasioned by the death of a close friend of her mother's. "How can one understand life if one does not conceive of it as being each individual's work on the spirit, a spirit which might well be called the Holy Ghost. Some do this with more fervency, others with less. But everyone, even the smallest person, contributes his mite. The talent and effort shown by Mrs. Rassow were produced by energy and no little struggling. [...] I held Mrs. Rassow in higher esteem than any other woman in Bremen. I suppose I would have told her this one day. I might have been able to do so had she lived longer, for I feel that certain dividing walls which Worpswede has set up between me and the world are now falling down. [...] I would also wish that Mrs. Rassow could have been there to experience my developing into something worthwhile. This would have been my simplest way of revealing myself to her. Because I am going to be something worthwhile. I myself cannot see how great or how small it will be, but it will be something self-contained. This steadfast rushing towards the goal is the finest thing in life. There is nothing else like it. If I sometimes appear not to be giving much love, then I ask you to remember that I am myself rushing forward the whole time, resting only occasionally so that I can once again rush towards the goal. My energies are being concentrated on this one thing. I do not know whether it may be called egoism. Whatever the case, it is the noblest kind of egoism[164]. I lay my head in your lap from which I came, and I thank you for my life. Your child."

She prepared very quietly for her departure for Paris. In a letter to Rainer Maria Rilke dated 17 February 1906, she very significantly observed (BT 434): "And now I do not know how to sign my name. I am not Modersohn, neither am I Paula Becker any more.

I am
myself,
and I hope to become myself more and more.
That is probably the final goal of all our struggles."

In the night after her husband's birthday, on 23 February 1906, she started out on her new life.

"... then also make a catch of fish"

Paris, 1906–1907

The Self-Portrait on My Sixth Wedding Anniversary (Ill. XXXII), painted in Paris, might be the heading preceding what happened next.

Paula Modersohn-Becker depicts herself semi-nude in this painting. The background is a sandy green, and its soft gleam is at its brightest around the human figure. It is enlivened by darker green spots. The artist is turned half right. Her head is held slightly inclined to one side. An amber necklace hangs down as far as her breasts. She holds her hands as if they were clasping something valuable. Her lower abdomen bulges as in a pregnancy. A cloth in bright blue hues surrounds her hips. Strangely, her left hand lies in front of the cloth without holding or gripping it. Delicate colour gradations softly mould the curves of her womanly body. At the lower right are the words: "I painted this at the age of thirty on my sixth wedding anniversary P.B."

This is something really new and unheard-of: a woman portrays herself in the nude and shows herself expecting a baby without really being pregnant. In these very weeks, Paula Modersohn-Becker had written to her husband that she did not want to have his child. So it is understandable that the literature interprets this painting in different ways.[165]

Some authors saw, in her nudity, auto-erotic tendencies on her part. The motif of pregnancy was interpreted as a projection of her wish to have children or as a reference to the painter's identification with the Christian type of the "mater gravida", the pregnant Virgin Mary.[166] According to Gisela Götte, the motif of the cloth indicates that Paula Modersohn-Becker was positively identified with the Venus femininity myth.[167]

To Doris Krininger, the portrait as a whole "demonstrates a self-examination, which poses as a subject for discussion the decision, not yet reached at that time, between life as an artist and existence as a married woman"[168].

The most fruitful remark seems to be that made by Christa Murken-Altrogge[169], in whose view Paula Modersohn-Becker is here presenting herself "as a vessel which wishes to produce a child, but equally also wishes to produce art.[170] The pregnancy hinted at here is a metaphor for the future and for evolution, for hope, but also for vulnerability."

In this interpretation, the authoress is referring to the symbolic, archetypal plane of the painting. Seen from this stratum of meaning, the child-to-be can also be seen as a symbol which often occurs in myths, fairy tales and dreams, and usually signifies growth and new beginning, but also the growth of the ego, or the birth of the personality pure and simple.

These differing attempts at interpretation show that the Self-Portrait

ON MY SIXTH WEDDING ANNIVERSARY is a many-sided work. It can probably scarcely be grasped in its entirety by merely referring to individual motifs. We shall probably come closer to the core of the statement being made if we always look at it in its artistic unity.

In this painting the artist portrays herself life-sized, as in a mirror. In contrast to many of her self-portraits, she pays attention here to real similarity as in a normal portrait.

The painting has a remarkable and diffuse brightness. This increases in indeterminateness as it goes down the picture, and the shapes of the body also become softer as they approach the cloth. The most clearly shaped part is the head with its hair which is here painted very darkly and resembles a cap. The artist's eyes are at the same level as the onlooker's. Her clear gaze with its restrained smile receives the onlooker's gaze with certainty. The narrow oval of the warm yellow amber necklace links the head with the area of the heart and breast. The right arm frames the entire upper part of the body in a bow and continues its movement to the left arm, which surrounds the lower abdomen. Taken together, both arms form the shape of an S which modulates the Gothic-looking S-shaped attitude of the entire human figure. The movement vibrates from the top downwards and ends in the gesture of the left hand.

The top edge of the cloth is at the same level as that hand. The cloth covers and delicately cloaks the body. In its white and sky blue, it is the most immaterial, spiritual part of the whole painting. The peculiar gesture of the left hand begins by taking the onlooker aback. Probably the most conclusive way of interpreting it is on the basis of Indian and esoteric knowledge. Paula Modersohn probably did not have such knowledge, but evidently herself had living experience of it.

Seen in this way, the gesture of the hand may be understood as a mandala, a symbol of the higher self. It indicates the original totality of life.[171] It lies before the chakra of the lower abdomen or the sexual chakra, the energetic place of sexuality and vital creative forces. The artist's right hand is on the chakra of the solar plexus. This chakra regulates the emotional energies. The amber necklace significantly surrounds two chakras simultaneously: it combines the heart chakra—the source of light and love—with the larynx chakra, the centre of creative expressiveness. Is it mere accident that, for the round pearls of the necklace, the artist used amber, the honey-coloured resin of trees in primeval times?

The inscription expressly states that Paula Modersohn-Becker painted this self-portrait on her sixth wedding anniversary. She signs it P.B., the initials of her maiden name, and she emphasizes that she is thirty years old. She had repeatedly determined to achieve something in the field of art before reaching this age.

Thus the painting might be understood as a nude and as a declaration of liberation. But this liberation is more than a release from marriage ties which have become a burden: it is a liberation enabling her to find herself, a liberation which she had expressed verbally in her letter to Rilke before departing for Paris: "I am myself...". "I am myself"—this applies to her as a woman, as an artist, as a person.

She seems to have about her the budding joy of a new day as she steps forth from the gently shining brightness of the greenish background; she does this with a totality which harbours all possibilities within itself and has not yet outlined individual hopes and wishes for the future. On the basis of her inner security and vitality, she is able to depict herself without protection in her womanly nudity, which refers neither to the polarity between the self and its surroundings nor to that between man and woman, but refers only to itself.

"Now I have left Otto Modersohn and I stand between my old life and my new one. What will happen in my new life? And how shall I develop in my new life? Everything must happen now," she wrote in her diary on arriving in Paris.[172]

Paula's departure was a serious blow to Otto Modersohn. His friends advised him to react by sternly "ordering" her to return to Worpswede.[173] But he preferred to write understanding letters to Paris: ". . . I loved everything about you and in you, [. . .], you were my measure in everything and for everything. Compared with you, what was there? I loved your soul, your feeling, like nothing else on this earth. Your art and your whole humanity were the dearest thing to me, and you know that too if you ask yourself" (6 April 1906). "Feel it, count on me, depend on me. Within me there resides no condemnation, but only the deepest feeling of which my entire being is capable. [. . .] Some are foolish, and the others are envious—I shall stand by you even if I have to go through hell. I have recognized the depths of your being and I know who you are" (11 April 1906.[174] But Paula always gave a similar answer to his urgent pleading: "Please let us not go into this matter at the moment, and let us allow some time to pass quietly. The answer which will then be found will be correct. I thank you for all your love. It is not cruelty and hardness on my part that is stopping me from relenting. It is hard for me too. I am doing it in the strong conviction that I should be tormenting you again in six months' time if I did not now examine myself enough. Try to get used to the possibility of our two lives going different ways."[175]

The Becker family also did not understand what Paula was concerned with. They tended to side with the husband she had abandoned. They were disappointed that the happiness in Worpswede, at which everyone had been so pleased, had been shattered. Indeed, Paula's method of procedure in that situation and that social environment was very unusual for those times.[176] Paula's mother could not even follow in her mind, let alone approve of, the step Paula had taken. But in a letter to her daughter she found words of sympathy, expressed with motherly love.[177] Paula answered by return[178]: "Yes, mother, I couldn't stand it any longer and I probably never shall be able to stand it again. It was all too cramped for me, and it was not what I need. It became less and less what I need." But in the very next sentence she is herself again, seeking and striving—neither a wife nor a daughter. "I'm now beginning a new life. Don't disturb me, let me get on with it. It's so wonderful. I lived through the last week as if intoxicated. I think I've accomplished something good."

Paula began by feeling very lonely in Paris. It was true that her favourite sister assisted her to some extent, but she too was unable to understand the step Paula had taken. Only Rilke was a great friend of hers. He too was in a sad frame of mind, because he had just parted company with Rodin, whose secretary he had been. Paula kept her head above water financially because Otto Modersohn generously sent her money every month.

She had a stroke of luck in her difficult situation. In mid-April she made the acquaintance of the sculptor Berhard Hoetger and his family. She had seen works by him in Bremen a year before, and then in Paris. Hoetger and his wife kindly took care of Paula, who had at first—and this is typical of her—concealed the fact that she was a painter. But when Hoetger learned of it through a chance remark, he did not give in until she finally showed him some paintings of hers.

And Hoetger recognized the quality of her paintings. He encouraged Paula to continue working. Herma Becker happened to witness this happy scene and wrote to her brother-in-law in Worpswede[179]: "Paula's work has now put her into a very elevated mood. Höxter (sic) looked at her pictures and they completely permeated him. 'Magnificent, very fine' etc., he kept on saying very quietly. And then he encouraged her and gave her the well-known, and sometimes actually necessary, impetus to go on with her painting. Now her little soul is liberated. I happened to drop in on them, and I saw and listened and was pleased at Paula's big eyes which were greedily, but at the same time meekly, drinking in all these revelations."[180]

Paula Modersohn-Becker now threw herself into her work with her "little soul liberated" and her self-confidence enhanced. The ideas which had accumulated and stored up over the last few years now made a path for themselves in an immense frenzy of creativity. "It is delightful to sleep amidst one's work. My studio is very light by moonlight. Whenever I woke up, I immediately used to leap from my bed and look at my work and it was the first thing I looked at in the mornings," she wrote to Worpswede[181].

She began to make a draught of fish and bring in the harvest. The sheer amount of physical work she accomplished over the next weeks and months is almost incomprehensible.

Apart from her independent work in her own studio, she again attended drawing courses at the Julian academy and anatomy courses at the École des Beaux-Arts. Twenty large nude drawings were produced in April alone. In her sketch books she drew drawings from nude models and sketches for compositions with human figures.

She also determined to learn a great deal more about painting: "Here my paintings look dark, like gravy. I must arrive at a much purer colour. I must learn to work the picture properly. I must do all sorts of things, and then something good may become of me. And you know, that is the final goal at which all my wishes and strivings will end."[182]

The PORTRAIT OF RAINER MARIA RILKE (Ill. XX) must have been produced in the period between 13 May and 2 June.[183] Its barrenness lends it a heartrending appearance. All the sympathetic and portrait-like features have been neturalized and reduced to simple and severe forms. The collar and beard support the head like a stiff shirt-cuff, and the basic shape of the head itself is geometrical. The eyes and mouth look as if they have been cut out of this shape. The large eyes have a peculiarly empty look. They are edged in red, as if the subject had been weeping for nights on end. The mouth, severely framed by the beard, resembles a deep red wound. It looks peculiarly rigid and undifferentiated.

The poet himself seemed affected by this, because he stopped sitting for Paula, explaining that he did not have the time. He never mentioned the portrait in the period that followed.

In this portrait, two aspects of Paula Modersohn-Becker's experiences with classical heads may be recognized. Firstly, she has here worked on certain ideas regarding shapes. "Forehead, eyes, mouth, nose, cheeks, chin, that's all. It sounds so simple, but it means a great deal," she noted down in Paris in 1903.

The second point is the concrete motif of the classical mask, which Paula

Modersohn is here clearly using.[184] She must have also found some classical masks in the Louvre when she was on her first search for simple things.

The mask was originally used in cultic contexts.[185] The classical mask associates its wearer with the gods and the dead. The individual human countenance is transformed by the mask into a general and collective phenomenon.

Accordingly, Paula Modersohn-Becker was not painting the countenance of Rilke the person, but the poet's face as a type. In this mask-like portrait she was evidently calling upon the poet to be a receptacle for universal validity, to be the proclaimer of primary words pure and simple, just as she herself wished to write "runic characters"—primary signs—in her paintings.

Rilke's reaction shows that he was hurt by being called upon in this way. During the years of their friendship, from 1900 onwards, they had repeatedly talked of such connections. Thus he may have sensed that he was being mildly criticized in this painting. Paula Modersohn, with her unerring instinct, had recognized weaknesses in their very first encounter: "He read us his poems, delicate and full of premonition. Sweet and pale."[186] Later, about a month before her death, she wrote the following lines to Rainer Maria Rilke, which are also to be understood in this sense: "I have just read your essay about Rodin in "Kunst und Künstler" and I was pleased at it. I believe that work is simpler the more mature it becomes. It seems to me that the delicately exuberant young man is disappearing, and that the real man is arising and using fewer words to say more."[187]

Basically, Rilke was always going on visits to Paula Becker. Richard Pettit wrote on this subject[188]: "In time, the figure of Cézanne gained an almost mystical greatness for Rilke. And as far as Rilke was concerned, Paula Modersohn-Becker, after her early death, moved closer and closer towards Cézanne." A year after her death, Rilke wrote a "requiem for a female friend". They contain some inimitably apposite words on her nature and her art:

"For this you understood: the full fruits.
You laid them down before you, on a dish
And conterposed the weight of them in colours.
And as you saw the fruits, so too the women
And saw the children too, from inward driven
Into those same shapes of their own Being.
And likewise saw yourself at last a fruit,
And took yourself from out your clothes, and then
Before the mirror stood, and drew within yourself
But for your gaze which, big, remained without,
Not saying: This am I; but more: This is.
So was your gaze in sum uncurious
And unpossessing, of poverty so true
It no longer wanted you: so sacred."

The requiem ends with a request to her:

"Do not return. If you can bear it, then
Be dead among the Dead. The Dead are busy.
But help me thus, that you be not distracted,
Help me as oft remote things help: within me."

The PORTRAIT OF LEE HOETGER (Ill. XXIV) was probably painted in July 1906[189]. Its colours are enchanting, and it shows the range of styles covered by this artist, who is here turning into art the impressions created by naive painting, such as is found in the works of "Douanier" Henri Rousseau.

Behind the cheerful naïvety of the human figure, flowers and butterflies there lies concealed a highly differentiated treatment of shapes and colours, of a kind which a reproduction cannot begin to show. In particular, several layers of colour are laid one above the other in the golden sky. This gives the colours an uninterruptedly pure and luminous appearance. This richness of nuance is best seen in the shoulder area of Mrs. Hoetger's dress. The pained and worried look on her face contrasts with the carefree nature of the overall arrangement.

The painting of the Sisters (1906; Ill. XXI) is built up on contrasts. Gentle colours and a softly dabbing painting method give rise to an impression of stillness, but it is a stillness full of artistic tension.

The independence of the two sisters finds expression in the contrasts in the form and content of this painting. The taller of the two is standing in severe profile. Her blonde hair and light complexion accord with her white dress. Her narrow eyes seem to be looking inwards. Her younger sister, with her white-dotted blue dress and her dark face and hair, faces the onlooker frontally, looking at him with her large brown eyes. She snuggles up to the larger figure, seeking protection. The sisters are holding one another by the shoulder. This crossing of their arms means that the younger sister's dark arm lies on the elder sister's white dress and that the latter's light hand is on the smaller girl's blue dress.

All contrasts of form, colour and attitude are closely related to one another, so that the two sisters melt into a single figure, a unity that radiates warmth. A silvery-grey background surrounds the two of them, creating throughout the picture a velvet clayey impression which unites the contrasts and is itself livened up by a few red accents.

Apart from her untiring work, Paula Modersohn-Becker enjoyed the city of Paris to the full. She walked about the town with her sketch book, recording Parisian life in some spontaneous, incisive drawings.[190] Here too, she was not so much noting down her own personal impressions, but rather what the city had to offer by way of beautiful architecture and interrelated forms (see Ill. 26, 27).

Otto Modersohn came to Paris at Whitsun. Paula was relieved when he departed again. But they had agreed that he would spend a fairly long period in Paris in autumn in order to see whether they would be able to live together again. She worked all through the summer. On 3 September Paula wrote to Worspwede and asked her husband to agree to a divorce. A few days later she retracted this decision, having been induced to do so by her friend Bernard Hoetger. Feminists have criticized him for giving this advice.[191] But this sculptor, experienced in the struggle for existence, had sympathetically realised that Paula would never be mentally or physically able to earn her own living on a permanent basis. He also knew that she was not prepared to give up her artistic activities in order to earn money. But she could not live on her pictures.

So Otto Modersohn came to Paris, and the couple spent a "delightful, harmonious"[192] winter there in 1906/07. Otto Modersohn largely gave up his own work, and made every effort to ensure that Paula could paint undisturbed.[193] On the other hand, the letters Paula wrote to her friends sound somewhat resigned and subdued. In them she repeatedly asks for love and understanding. In the final analysis, she knew that it was only by letting her husband take her under his wing that she could find the quiet and security she needed in order to continue working.

26
Parisian Horse Bus
c. 1906
Charcoal, 29.5 x 21.5 cm
Privately owned

A letter dated 17 November 1906 to her friend Clara Rilke-Westhoff reveals something of Paula's situation: "I shall return to my former life, but with certain alterations. I myself have changed: I am somewhat more independent and no longer full of too many illusions. I noticed this summer that I am not the kind of woman who can live on her own. Apart from the constant concern about money, my very freedom would tempt me away from my goal of self-fulfilment. And I would so much like to arrive at the point where I can create something which is a realisation of my own self. Only time will tell whether this is a brave act on my part. The main thing is to find the quiet I need to work in, and in the long run it will be at Otto Modersohn's side that I shall best be able to find this quiet."[194] In this connection, H.Chr. Kirsch[195] remarks, probably correctly, that her decision to return to Worspwede was partly based on an "inner independence which she had by now attained".

During these weeks, in November 1907, some of her works were exhibited in the Kunsthalle in Bremen, and Gustav Pauli's favourable review ended as fol-

27
Hooded Child in Paris Street
c. 1906
Charcoal, 29.5 x 22 cm
Privately owned

lows: "But let it be said that we may consider ourselves lucky to be able to call a talent as great as Paula Modersohn's our own. This artist has been living in Paris for some time, and the influence of the incomparable culture to be found there, particularly that of Cézanne, has not visibly harmed her."[196] Paula replied to this as follows in a letter to her sister Milly[197]: "That review gave me more gratification than joy. [...] But the review was good for my exhibition in Bremen and it may cause my departure from Worpswede to be seen in a different light. Otto and I are coming home again in spring. He is very affecting in his love. [...] My present attitude is like this: if dear God will once again permit me to create something beautiful, I shall be pleased and contented if I have somewhere where I can work quietly, and I shall be grateful for the portion of love which has fallen to my share. If only I can stay healthy and don't die too early."

While still in Paris she made two very different statements concerning motherhood.

One of them is the MOTHER LYING WITH CHILD (1906; Ill. XXII). The two are lying unclothed on a white sheet. The mother's mature physicality finds expression in a soft three-dimensionality which draws its strength from within: every part of the warm-coloured body surface seems to know the central point of the body. This central point is visible towards the outside, being the mother's navel. The child has the same plump roundness in its shapes. It is turned towards its mother, and like her it is lying on its side with its legs pulled up slightly.

Four sketches show the route pursued by the artist in arriving at this statement of motherhood (see Ill. 28). The union between mother and child is warm-hearted and almost playful.

All individual traits have been removed from the painting. The mother's head accordingly appears two-dimensional and stylized. The posture of the two bodies has lost all personal tenderness, but without becoming cold or distant. It is a quiet and plain togetherness. The child's little head lies on the mother's right arm. The mother's left arm is not clasped around the child in the traditional motherly gesture. Instead it bends slightly around the child's head.

The many physical contacts between the large figure and the small express closeness and safety. Between mother and child there is a unity which conceals release and separation within itself.

The child accordingly has a blanket of its own. The small white blanket looks more luminous and less worn-out than the large white sheet which becomes shadowy towards the top. May this be understood symbolically as a symbol of a path in life which has not yet been described?

By way of the sketches and two versions (they have survived only in photographs) of the motif, Paula Modersohn-Becker arrived at a form whose validity extends beyond the individuals depicted. This form depicts the act by which life puts itself forth. The temporal dimensions of motherhood—pregnancy, birth, separation—are symbolically combined in a timeless present moment. It might be said that an archetype, as in Jungian depth psychology, is here given life. This refers us to a level of meaning at which the painting still has an effect today.[198]

Some time before painting her picture MOTHER LYING WITH CHILD, Paula Modersohn-Becker had begun making the "catch of fish" she once spoke of. Now she is writing in "runic characters". The German word "Rune" (mean-

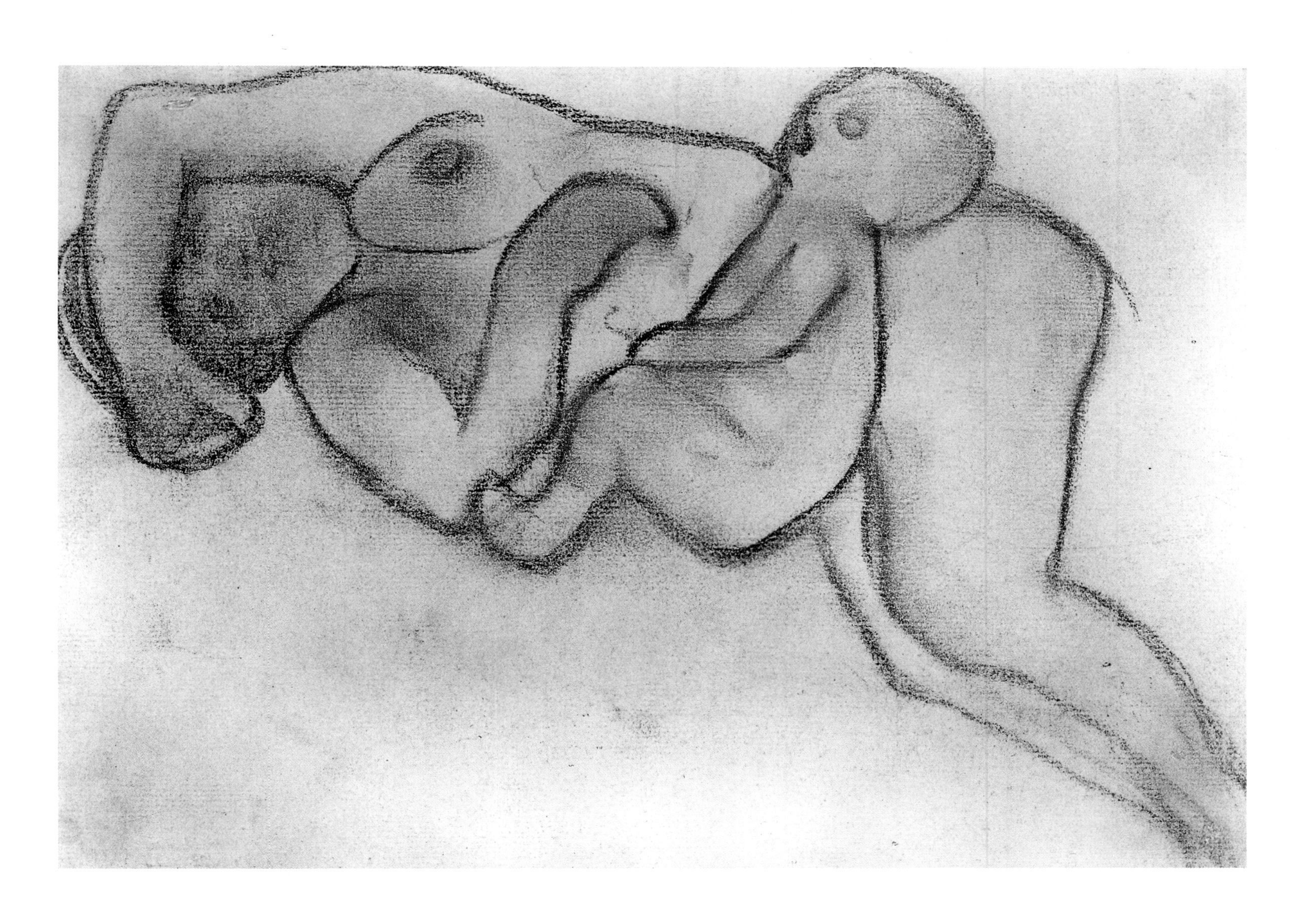

28
Mother Lying With Seated Child
1906
Charcoal, 21.5 x 31.3 cm
Hamburg Kunsthalle

ing the same as the English "rune") is etymologically related to "raunen" ("to whisper"), and is based on a root which means "secret". Thus the term "runic characters" refers aptly to the difficulties frequently encountered by the onlooker: while the symbolists who were highly regarded by this painter display the symbolic and allegorical meaning of their work in an unmistakable and sometimes almost obtrusive fashion, the language of Paula Modersohn-Becker is reserved and withdrawn. It expresses itself solely by artistic means.

The subject of motherhood is deal with entirely differently in the painting Mother Kneeling With Child (1907; Ill. XXIII).

The mother kneels on a blanket, as in an ancient statue. She clasps in her arms the child peacefully sucking at her breast. The composition is built up on the contrast produced by the various artistic means employed.

The first item that strikes the onlooker is the glowing strength of the colours. The turquoise in the background gleams almost exotically above the dark green of the stylized foliage plants. The brightest and coolest part of the picture is the blanket. Around it, warm-coloured fruits are distributed on a grey ground. Their shapes and colours are related to the mother's nipple and to the child's mouth and cheek, and they may be understood as being symbols of fertility.

The three-dimensional bodies of mother and child contrast, in a manner rich in tension, with the two-dimensional background. The bodily forms are worked in both light and dark surfaces, so that they are illuminated but also cast shadows. They are depicted with a severely cubical reduction which points to later cubist paintings by Picasso. Instead of the fine colour gradations of the picture in Bremen, we here find sharply contrasting surfaces and strips, which are though in themselves artistically treated. In this process some sections arise which look positively abstract (e.g. the mother's neck and shoulder region). The cool bluish-violet shades, along with the turquoise and green of the background, emphasize the warm colourfulness of the human bodies. Beige, pink, and various nuances of red including earthy brown hues, are used for the bodies.

The differing degrees of brightness and warmth in the colours are not the only contrast in the picture. The column-like erectness of the mother also opposes the soft snuggling of the child.

The centre of the painting, in terms of both composition and content, is at the point where the mother holds the child that is sucking at her breast. Strangely, the mother's arms and shoulders form a pentagon. The crystalline character of this form contrasts with the roundness of the light-coloured blanket.

A deep symbolism seems to lie concealed in the pentagon and the round disc: the number five was regarded in classical times as a symbol of wedding and synthesis. To the Chinese it was the number for the harmonic combination of yin and yang, while in Hinduism it was the number of the vital principle.

The disc shape of the blanket might in turn be seen as a mandala, the symbol of the original totality of life. This interpretation lends the strong brightness of the blanket a particular meaning. The round blanket also carries mother and child like an island and strongly supports the blend of the contrasting artistic means used in the painting.

In this picture, Paula Modersohn-Becker uses the topic of motherhood on several planes of meaning: this motherhood is a unifying element, but also conceals within itself the idea of separation and polarity. In this regard this painting resembles the one in Bremen. But in contrast to the latter, the separation is here experienced almost painfully: the mother faces away from the light. Her head is so much in shadow as to be almost lifeless. Her dark eyes are not directed towards the child, but towards an undefined object beyond the left-hand edge of the picture. All warmth and liveliness are concentrated in the baby, who is completely turned towards the brightness. The child seems to look trustingly upwards and to the right, as if contemplating a bright future.

Runic characters

Worpswede, 1907

When Otto and Paula Modersohn returned to Worpswede in Easter 1907, Paula was expecting a baby. The last circle of her life was beginning to close.

Her new function, for which she had been longing for so long, was felt by her to be a fulfilment and an elevation. According to Otto Modersohn, the bitterness of the year 1906 "had completely fallen from her; she was full of dedication and gratitude towards me, grateful that I had not abandoned her in 1906, that year of storm and stress, but had helped her through that time"[199]. Paula's mother went to Worpswede on Ascension Day 1907, and wrote to Paula's sister Herma of her time with the Modersohns: "[. . .] I would not have begrudged you any of it, especially not the still harmony of the hearts which, mentioned by no one, permeated our harmless chat like the music of the spheres. [. . .] I never had the feeling that there was anything patched-up and repaired about it: one felt safety and lucidity everywhere."[200]

She painted only a little in the summer months preceding childbirth. But that little shows an immense compactness of form and statement. Her SELF-PORTRAIT WITH CAMELLIA TWIG (Ill. XXX) shows the spiritual dimensions into which this artist advanced in the last year of her life. It is notable that it was confiscated in 1937 as being "degenerate".

This self-portrait deals, in both form and content, with Egyptian mummy portraits from Fayoum.[201] Paula Modersohn discovered these portraits in Paris in 1903. In February 1907, her husband gave her, as a thirty-first birthday present, a folder containing reproductions of such portraits, which she found "very strange and characteristic"[202]. It is possible that this birthday present inspired her to paint the self-portrait with camellia twig. If so, it was painted in spring 1907 and was one of her very last self-portraits.

What induced this artist to depict herself in this way: she who had such a fear of death, of early death?

Egyptian mummy portraits were usually painted while the person depicted was still alive. After he died the portrait was wrapped up and placed on the mummy's face. The purpose of this custom was to retain the deceased person's facial features so that he might live on as an individual being after his death.

Paula Modersohn-Becker dealt with matters of death and dying throughout her life, as the evidence she gives concerning herself reveals. She evidently regarded death as the dark brother of an intense life lived in joy. Now, in view of her pregnancy and impending childbirth, such ideas may have gained an additional relevance.

In her self-portrait, Paula Modersohn-Becker makes use of the rounded form of the Egyptian portraits, by using strips on the right and left to set off the whole height of the picture surface, turning that surface slightly in towards the centre of the picture. This creates a kind of inner frame, which makes the picture's shape seem even taller and narrower than it is already. Even without this addition, the self-portrait has a more stretched shape than its Egyptian models. In contrast to the latter, the painter also includes so much of her bust that it takes up half the surface of the picture.

The painter, looking dark, stands before the gleaming blue of the background, a blue passing into turquoise. This is the colour of the sky, remoteness and infinity. In symbolic terms, it is the colour of the spirit and of the letting-go which is part of the dying process.[203]

The gleaming becomes brighter still around the head and neck. This makes the human figure look even darker, and the brown hues of her flesh tint gain in warmth. The light of the background is absorbed into the outer corners of the large gazing eyes, which shine from an unfathomable depth, clear-sighted and knowing. The other sensual organs—the nose and ears—also seem to be wide open.

To the deep seriousness of the eyes, the mouth adds a smile, cordial warmth and female attractiveness. The roundness of the lower lip also takes up the round and oval forms of the eyes and the area around them, and leads on to the oval of the chin and the roundness of the necklace.

Here, in the physical centre of the picture, the necklace and the topmost leaf of the camellia twig cross one another. The twig with its green leaves grows upwards in front of the artist's heart and breast area, held by two fingers—larger than life and only hinted at—of her right hand. The size and brightness of this area correspond to the blue of the upper half of the picture. This central area is barely complete, but it is vitally warm and earthly and comes closest to the onlooker, contrasting in this with the immaterial remoteness of the blue section.

The ways in which this self-portrait deviates from Egyptian mummy portraits give an insight into its deep significance and symbolism. The excessively narrow and tall shape, the strips at the sides, and the vertical commenced by the camellia twig and continuing along the nose, the parting of the hair, and a black line—all this induces the onlooker to let his gaze move repeatedly upwards and downwards:

Underneath, in the region of the middle of the heart, the artist's hand holds the camellia twig which is in the shape of a mandala.[204] The twig, the embodiment of growing life, grows past the collarbone—which is emphasized and resembles a dish—and goes up into more compact areas. In the centre of the picture's surface, the twig touches the artist's neck at the point where the larynx, being the organ of speech, and the neck chakra, being the energetic place of artistic self-expression, are both located.

The dark gleaming of the eyes draws the onlooker's gaze upwards into the area of maximum compactness, where transcendency is visible in the artist's gaze and smile. Thus this painting addresses a plane of existence where the polarities of nearness and remoteness, growing and passing away, permanence and transience, life and death, seem to have been eliminated.[205]

A comparison of two paintings depicting "Dreebeen", a female poorhouse inmate, illustrates the transformation undergone by the familiar figures known from earlier pictures.

The "Dreebeen" in the picture called OLD POORHOUSE WOMAN (c. 1905; Ill. XXVI) is sitting in a garden and looking massive and voluminous. The trees, animals, meadow and hedge have been assigned to her as attributes marking out the rustic framework of her everyday life. Her rough hands lie quietly in her lap. She is looking ahead of herself, quiet and pensive. The whole picture is bathed in soft reddish-green colours.

The "Dreebeen" in the late painting OLD POORHOUSE WOMAN WITH GLASS BOTTLE (1907; Ill. XXVII) has been elevated as if into a magic realm. She is now close to the onlooker, and her dark appearance is built up against a suggestive-looking evening sky, whose warm golden colour changes over, as it moves upwards, into gleaming turquoise hues interspersed with red and blue. The glow of the sky penetrates through the edge of the straw hat the old woman is wearing, and transforms it into a kind of materialized nimbus. This gleam continues in the greyish-violet of the bonnet and the ribbon, and glows darkly once again in the old woman's eyeballs and lower lip.

The upper part of "Dreebeen"'s body has been given a warm red form, which seems to have been driven into it from within. Its three-dimensional shapes grow from a bluish skirt, covered with circles and spots. From the deep green of a meadow, poppy plants strive upwards against the sky: the poppy heads are black silhouettes, while the blooms retain their own red luminous strength. The decorations in the plants and in the skirt are in contrast to the rest of the picture, an impression reinforced by the black outlines and by the light-blue surfaces which are seen amidst the tangle of plants and appear to be unmotivated. Their brightness corresponds to that of the sky, while as a motif they are probably meant to be a neck for the glass bottle.

The inverted glass bottle is placed opposite "Dreebeen", and not merely by way of a formal correspondence. There was a glass bottle in the Modersohns' garden, and Paula repeatedly used it as a formally inspiring motif in her paintings and drawings. In the present painting the bottle may refer to a symbolic level of meaning attained by the picture as a whole. As a vessel, it might be a symbol of femininity. At the same time, being an earth-coloured background for poppy blooms and poppy heads, it reflects the old woman's world and activity. In Minoan Crete and classical Greece, poppy heads were attributes of earth goddesses and fertility goddesses. The poppy is also a medicinal plant leading to intoxication and sleep.[206] The foxglove, which the old woman is holding in her hand like a sceptre, is also a medicinal plant.

The old woman seen in OLD POORHOUSE WOMAN, the earlier picture, now in Wuppertal, has in the late painting been transformed into a personality who, with her lumpy and defiant facial expression, observes in a wide-awake, knowing way. Paula Modersohn-Becker has brought her close to primitive beings such as earth mothers and fertility goddesses, or else she has moved her into a magic world where women have secret knowledge and curative powers, as witches formerly did. The OLD PEASANT WOMAN (1907; Ill. XXIX) sits on a chair in front of a kind of parapet; she seems to have been detached from earthly things but is nonetheless fully present physically.

The features which urged the previous picture towards many colours and much articulation are more restrained here. The harmony of colours in the picture is defined by the warm living flesh tints of the face and hands and by the blue of the dress, which shines forth from the darkness. The dress looks like an abstract composition which has been folded so as to fit on to the picture surface and consists of surfaces in shades of blue with black outlines. These surfaces point towards the black cuff as towards a centre. It is there that the peasant woman's hands are crossed over her breast.

This is an equivocal gesture. It expresses devotion, preparedness, humility and spiritualization. It is the gesture with which, according to the Christian pictorial tradition, the Virgin Mary received the Angel's message.

In the old woman's lap there are three simple blooms gleaming like little suns. The old woman's blue eyes are as deep as a lake. They are looking inwards and seem to perceive the glow at the back of the picture. Shadowy tendrils with leaves in the shape of hearts emerge from this brightness. The whitish-blue light seems to belong to a different, spiritual sphere. It gathers around the peasant woman's head like an aura.

In this picture of a woman, Paula Modersohn-Becker has succeeded in using colour and form to lend expression and life to such phenomena as "immanent transcendency" (Dürckheim) and "diaphanousness" (Gebser).

Paula Modersohn-Becker wrote the following to Bernard Hoetger about the pictures painted that summer: "I have done little work this summer and I do not know whether you will like any of that little. The conception of the items depicted is probably the same overall. But they now manifest themselves differently in the pictures. I would like to show the rushing, full, exciting nature of the colours, the mighty factor in them. The pictures I did in Paris are too cool, too solitary and empty. They are a reaction to a superficial period of disquiet, and they aim to make a large and simple impression."[207]

These lines show that she has now reached a new plane from which she assesses the paintings she produced in Paris from a critical distance. She seems to be aware of the different character of her new paintings. The letter to Hoetger ends with some strange words from which there speaks an inner simplicity: "I can only ask, over and over again: Dear God, make me devout, so that I may go to Heaven." She told her mother that she must paint more flowers.[208]

Paula Modersohn-Becker painted herself one last time, this time as a SELF-PORTRAIT WITH TWO FLOWERS IN MY RAISED HAND, dating from 1907 (Ill. XXXI). She chooses the narrow vertical format this time too but, in contrast to the SELF-PORTRAIT WITH CAMELLIA TWIG, she here makes an impression of complete earthly presence. Her eyes look directly at the onlooker. Her face radiates fulfilment and joy. Her right hand is on her swelling body. Almost triumphantly, she holds in her left raised hand a twig with two simple blooms. This double bloom can be interpreted as a symbol of duality, the duality of mother and child[209], but also in general terms as the polarity between the ego and its opposite number.

In the SELF-PORTRAIT ON MY SIXTH WEDDING ANNIVERSARY, the birth of a new personality and of a new ego had taken place inwardly, and it found expression in that painting. This now also took place outwardly. On 2 November 1907, Paula Modersohn-Becker gave birth to a little girl named Mathilde. About two weeks later, on 20 November, when she was allowed to get up for the first time, she suddenly collapsed and died of an embolism. Her last words were: "Wie schade" ("What a shame").

There was a last picture on her easel: FLOWER STILL LIFE WITH SUNFLOWER AND MALLOWS (1907; Ill. XXVIII). It is a painting of the fulness of life, captured in autumn flowers. The sunlight in them has matured to a deep glow. But the flowers have been cut and harvested.

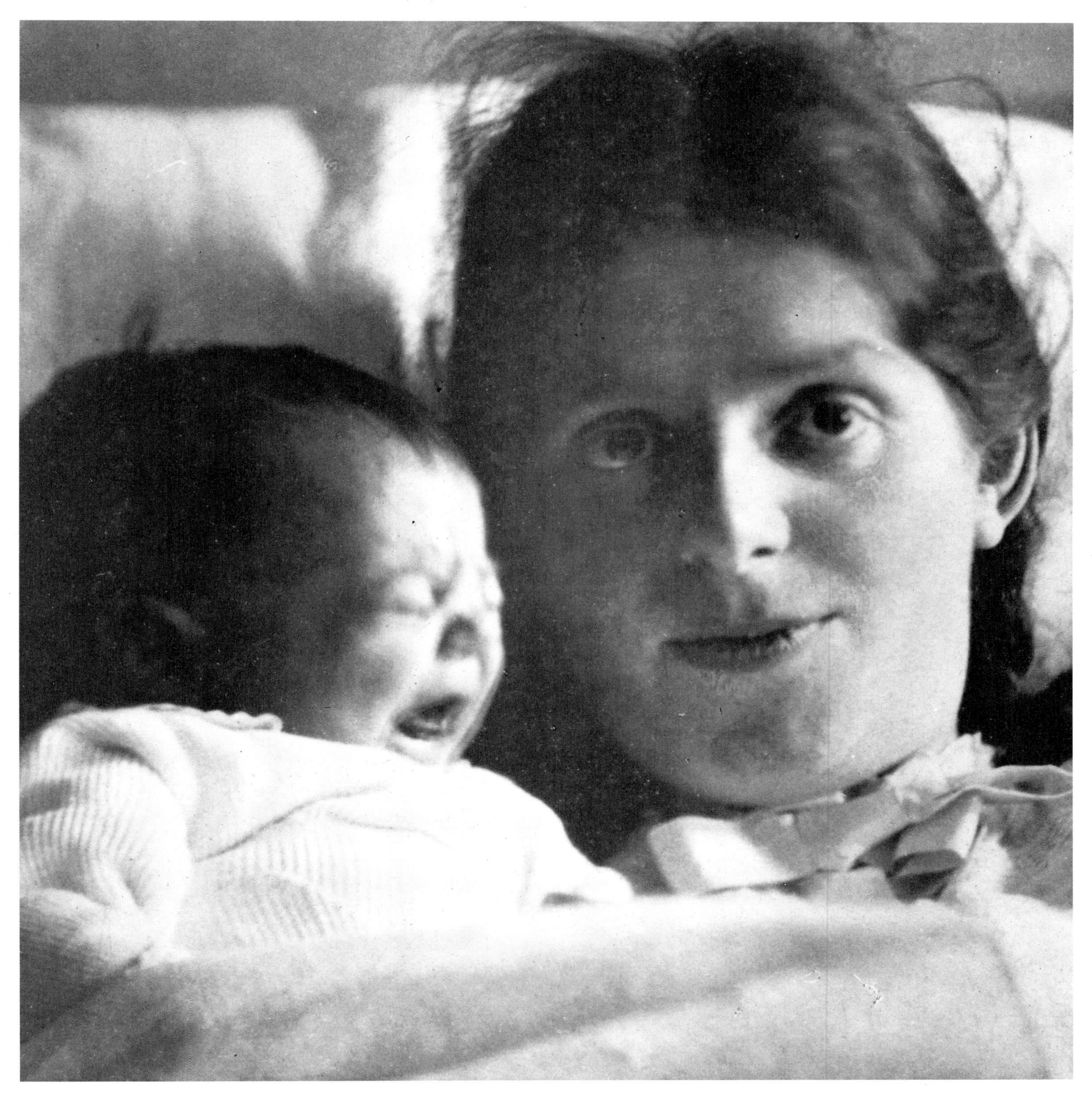

29
Paula Modersohn-Becker with her daughter
Mathilde
November 1907

Notes

1 In Rolf Hetsch (ed.): Paula Modersohn-Becker. Ein Buch der Freundschaft. Berlin 1932, p. 60
2 Günter Busch: Paula Modersohn – Heute: In: Paula Modersohn-Becker zum 100. Geburtstag. Gemälde – Zeichnungen – Graphik. Catalogue of exhibition at Kunsthalle. Bremen 1976, (Introduction, p. 2)
3 A.E. Brinckmann: Spätwerke großer Meister. Frankfurt 1925, p. 19
4 Richard Hamann: Die deutsche Malerei vom Rokoko bis zum Expressionismus. Leipzig und Berlin 1925, p. 465 f.
5 Carl Einstein: Die Kunst des 20. Jahrhunderts. Berlin 1926, p. 127
6 Gustav Pauli: Paula Modersohn-Becker. Leipzig 1919 According to Christian Modersohn (November 1987), Pauli did not consult Otto Modersohn before writing his monograph. I should like at this point to thank all those who generously assisted in the work on this book: Mrs. Tille Modersohn, Mr. Christian Modersohn and Mr. Wolfgang Werner of the Paula Modersohn-Becker foundation in Bremen.
7 Eine Künstlerin, Paula Modersohn-Becker Briefe und Tagebücher. Edited by S.D. Gallwitz on behalf of the Kestner-Gesellschaft e.V. Hanover. Bremen 1917
8 Cf. Hans-Christian Kirsch: Worpswede. Die Geschichte einer deutschen Künstlerkolonie. Munich 1987, p. 217 ff.
9 Paula Modersohn-Becker in Briefen und Tagebüchern. Edited by Günter Busch and Liselotte von Reinken. Frankfurt am Main 1979 (abbreviation used in this book: BT)
10 According to Günter Busch: Paula Modersohn-Becker, Malerin Zeichnerin. Frankfurt am Main 1981, p. 67, Paula's only "follower" was Hans Meyboden, a pupil of Kokoschka.
11 C.G. Jung: Sigmund Freud als kulturhistorische Erscheinung (1932). In: C.G. Jung: Über das Phänomen des Geistes in Kunst und Wissenschaft. Collected Works, vol. XV, Olten and Freiburg im Breisgau (4) 1984, p. 44
12 Stanislaw Przybyszewski: Das Werk des Edvard Munch, Berlin 1894, p. 16 and 4; quoted after Anni Carlsson: Edvard Munch. Leben und Werk. Stuttgart/Zurich 1984, p. 42
13 Cf. C.G. Jung: Über die Beziehungen der analytischen Psychologie zum dichterischen Kunstwerk (1922). In: Collected Works, vol. XV, (4) 1984, p. 95
14 Letter to Rainer Maria Rilke dated 25.10.1900; BT 240
15 Cf. Busch 1981, p. 20
16 29.7.1892; BT 39
17 7.8.1892; BT 40
18 These sketching hours mean that Paula Becker kept to the dilettante tradition. On the details of this and her artistic training, see Anne Röver: Laienzeichen – Akademisches Zeichnen – Freies Zeichnen. In: Paula Modersohn-Becker. Das Frühwerk. Catalogue of exhibition held at Bremen Kunsthalle. 1985 (no page numbering)
19 22.9.1892; BT 44 f.
20 21.11.1892; BT 50 f.
21 Cf. Röver in Bremen catalogue 1985 (p. 8 and 10)
22 5.5.1893; BT 60 f.
23 Cf. Tamar Garb: Frauen des Impressionismus. Die Welt des farbigen Lichts. Stuttgart, Zurich 1987, p. 6–9
24 Cf. Paula Modersohn-Becker, mit Selbstzeugnissen und Bilddokumenten dargestellt von Liselotte von Reinken. Hamburg 1983, p. 21 f.
25 Letter from Leipzig dated 3.7.1896; BT 83. It is notable that he signed this letter "Your old misanthropist".
26 14.7.1897; BT 99
27 28.10.1897; BT 107
28 To her parents, 7.5.1897; BT 98
29 She travelled to Vienna and Dresden in 1897, and visited Max Klinger in Leipzig in April 1898.
30 Before 18 May 1896; BT 81 f.
31 Willi Baumeister: Das Unbekannte in der Kunst. Stuttgart 1947, p. 31
32 Baumeister 1947, p. 33
33 Cf. Conrad Fiedler: Der Ursprung der künstlerischen Tätigkeit (1887). In: Schriften über Kunst. New edition, Cologne 1988, p. 173
34 Cf. also Doris Krininger: Modell – Malerin – Akt. Über Suzanne Valadon und Paula Modersohn-Becker. Darmstadt and Neuwied 1986
35 26.4.1893; BT 59
36 Cf. Kirsch 1987, p. 17 ff. and Kirsch: Otto Modersohn und Worpswede. In: Otto Modersohn – Die Zeichnungen. Exhibition catalogue. Münster 1988, p. 19–33
37 27.4.1895; BT 65
38 On the concept of "non-perspective" seeing, see Jean Gebser: Ursprung und Gegenwart. Vol. 1. Stuttgart 1949 and 1953; paperback edition 1973, p. 26 f.
39 24.7.1897; BT 101
40 24.7.1897; BT 102
41 R.M. Rilke: Worpswede. Fritz Mackensen, Otto Modersohn, Fritz Overbeck, Hans am Ende, Heinrich Vogeler. In: Complete Works, vol. V. Frankfurt am Main 1965, p. 27
42 Diary entry of 24.1.1899; BT 152
43 19.1.1899; BT 151
44 Letter to Paris dated April 1900; quoted after BT 211
45 In his monograph on Worpswede. In: Complete Works, vol. V. 1965, p. 28/29
46 In the following, see Röver in Bremen catalogue 1985, chapter on Worpswede 1898/99
47 BT 163 f.
48 Fritz Mackensen in: Hetsch 1932, quoted after Bremen catalogue 1985, note 108
49 Letter to her father dated 2.3.1899; BT 158
50 Letter to her parents dated 12.2.1899; BT 155
51 15.11.1899; BT 170
52 Quoted after BT 171
53 Pauli 1919, p. 14
54 Busch 1981, p. 21 ff.
55 Quoted after BT 172
56 E.g. criticism of 1895 exhibition in "Journal des Artistes": "The nightmarish visions seen in these monstrosities painted in oils exceed today the degree of poor jesting permitted by law." Quoted after Christoph Wetzel: Paul Cézanne. Leben und Werk. Stuttgart-Zürich 1984, p. 68
57 Quoted after BT 173
58 Quoted after Otto Stelzer: Paula Modersohn. Berlin 1958, p. 10
59 17.1.1900; BT 191 and 522
60 Cf. also Gisela Götte in the exhibition catalogue: Paula Modersohn-Becker. Worpswede Paris. Clemens-Sels Museum, Neuss 1985, p. 9 f.
61 Cf. Busch 1981, p. 32 f.
62 Ibidem.
63 In: Buch der Freundschaft 1932, p. 43
64 Cf. Erwin Panofsky: Die Perspektive als 'symbolische Form'. In: Vorträge der Bibliothek Warburg, 1924/25. Leipzig-Berlin 1927, p. 258–330; printed in: Erwin Panofsky: Aufsätze zu Grundfragen der Kunstwissenschaft. Berlin (2) 1974, p. 99–167
65 Panofsky 1924/25, quoted according to reprint (2) 1974, p. 122
66 Stelzer 1958, p. 7
67 Walter Hess: Dokumente zum Verständnis der modernen Malerei. Hamburg 1956, (9) 1968, p. 12
68 Cf. Hess (9) 1968, p. 12
69 Fritz Schmalenbach: Impressionismus. Versuch einer Systematisierung. Lecture held in 1964; printed in Fritz Schmalenbach: Studien über Malerei und Malereigeschichte. Berlin 1972, p. 16
70 Schmalenbach 1964 (1972), p. 16
71 Cf. also Wolfgang Schöne: Das Licht in der Malerei. Berlin 1954, p. 198 ff.
72 Hess (9) 1986, p. 13
73 Joachim Gasquet: Cézanne (conversations). Paris 1921, German version Berlin 1930; quoted after Hess (9) 1968, p. 19
74 Jean Gebser: In der Bewährung. Zehn Hinweise auf das neue Bewusstsein. Berne, Munich 1962, p. 127

75 Gebser 1962, p. 132
76 Letter to O. and H. Modersohn, 29.2.1900; BT 203
77 Cf. also Stelzer 1958, p. 8, and Busch 1981, p. 36
78 Cf. also Busch 1981, p. 63
79 About 13.4.1900; BT 215
80 Diary entry of 2.7.1900; BT 229
81 Cf. v. Reinken 1983, p. 59
82 Diary entry of 24.2.1902; BT 311
83 On the dispute on Hoetger's designing the grave, see Kirsch 1987, p. 141 ff.
84 3.9.1900; BT 233
85 The paintings were whitewashed over in 1935 and only re-discovered a few years ago, in 1986.
86 Although Otto Modersohn regarded this date for the engagement as premature, he gave in to Paula's urging (according to the draft of Otto Modersohn's letter to Gustav Pauli on the publication of the first monograph dated 19.6.1919; printed in Christa Murken-Altrogge: Paula Modersohn-Becker. Leben und Werk. Cologne 1980, p. 177)
87 On the conflict between Mackensen and Modersohn and the collapse of the Worpswede artists' community, see Kirsch 1987, p. 121 ff.
88 Heinrich Vogeler in his "Erinnerungen"; see David Erlay: Künstler Kinder Kommunarden. Heinrich Vogeler und sein Barkenhoff. Fischerhude 1979, p. 48
89 "Schmargendorfer Tagebuch", in: Tagebücher aus der Frühzeit. Frankfurt am Main 1973, p. 237 (16.9.1900)
90 Cf. Busch 1981, p. 41
91 Cf. Busch 1981, p. 40
92 29.2.1900; BT 204
93 Another letter to the Modersohns, early May 1900; BT 222
94 Letter to Clara Rilke-Westhoff dated 13.5.1901; BT 299
95 Quoted after Hess (9) 1968, p. 31
96 Printed in Murken-Altrogge 1980, p. 117
97 7.2.1901; BT 281 f.
98 23.3.1901; BT 298
99 Quoted after BT 247
100 30.3.1902; BT 317
101 Diary entry of 2.5.1902; BT 319
102 Cf. Busch 1981, p. 28 ff.
103 7.7.1902; quoted after BT 326
104 The reference is to the painting "Study with glass ball and goat", 1902, Wuppertal, v.d. Heydt Museum
105 9.7.1902; quoted after BT 326. According to Christian Modersohn (November 1987), the correct reading is "Luft, Licht" ("air and light") and not "Lust, Liebe" ("desire and love").
106 18.2.1903; BT 340 f.
107 See Annemarie Krummacher's contribution in: Paula Modersohn-Becker. Ein Buch der Freundschaft. Revised version of 1932 edition, Fischerhude 1985, p. 49
108 Cf. also Murken-Altrogge 1980, p. 71
109 2.5.1902; BT 319
110 28.6.1902; BT 324
111 Stelzer 1958, p. 13
112 11.3.1902; quoted after Kirsch 1988, p. 30. The author properly observes (p. 32, note 2) that any investigations regarding Otto Modersohn's biography and his relationship with his second wife and his friends and colleagues from his earlier years will remain incomplete "until copies of all the surviving diaries, notebooks and letters of Otto Modersohn can be examined and compared with the sources known today".
113 1.12.1902; BT 330 f.
114 Also 1.12.1902; BT 331
115 14.2.1903; BT 337
116 Letter to Otto Modersohn dated 17.2.1903; BT 339
117 Anne Röver: Die Nachzeichnungen Paula Modersohn-Beckers. In: Niederdeutsche Beiträge 16, 1977, p. 211
118 Cf. Röver 1977, p. 208
119 15.2.1903; BT 337 f.
120 17.2.1903; BT 339
121 Diary entry of 25.2.1903; BT 345
122 Diary entry of 15.2.1903; BT 338
123 Letter to Otto Modersohn dated 14.2.1903; BT 335
124 To Otto Modersohn, 18.2.1903; BT 341
125 Diary entry of 20.2.1903; BT 344. As early as 1899, a diary entry (19.1.1899; BT 151) states: "I feel it in me like a faint tissue, a vibration, a beating of wings, a trembling rest, a holding of breath: when I can paint, I shall paint it."
126 Letter to B. Hoetger in summer 1907; BT 473
127 Letter to Kurt Becker dated 26.4.1900; BT 216
128 Letter to Otto Modersohn dated 15.1.1901; BT 269
129 Wassily Kandinsky in his essays of 1923–1943, quoted after Hess (9) 1968, p. 87
Comparable remarks can also be found in Jawlensky. On this subject, Clemens Weiler (Alexej Jawlensky, Cologne 1959, p. 32) writes: "Jawlensky, who always based his work on concrete ideas, gave a description saying that the coloured apples arranged to form a still life were not apples to him any longer. Instead, when they merged with the colour of the background, the apples became a harmony which was interwoven with coloured dissonances and sounded like music in his eye combining with his particular mood to form a unity."
130 23.3.1903; quoted after BT 359
131 20.4.1903; BT 360 f.
132 Hamann 1925, p. 465
133 25.12.1900; BT 253
134 Quoted after Murken-Altrogge 1980, p. 117
135 26.9.1903; for a detailed description see Kirch 1987, p. 122 ff., which also includes the complete quotation; incomplete quotation also in BT, p. 370
136 Kirsch 1987, p. 124
137 15.4.1904; BT 374
138 15.4.1904; BT 376
139 23.2.1905 to Otto Modersohn; BT 397 f.
140 To Otto Modersohn, 22.3.1905; BT 412
141 Letter dated Good Friday, 21.4.1905, to Herma Becker; BT 416 ff.
142 Quoted after Kirsch 1987, p. 129
143 Cf. Peter J. Harke: Stilleben von Paula Modersohn-Becker. Worpswede 1985, p. 98
144 Cf. Busch 1981, p. 63
145 Cf. Harke 1985, p. 32
146 Carl Georg Heise: Paula Modersohns Wiederkehr. 1957. In: Der gegenwärtige Augenblick. Reden und Aufsätze aus vier Jahrzehnten. Berlin 1960, p. 157
147 Harke 1985, p. 63
148 Stelzer 1958, p. 18, and Busch 1981, p. 62
149 Cf. also Harke 1985, p. 92
150 "The strength with which an object is registered (still lifes, portraits or fanciful creations): therein lies beauty in art." Diary entry in Paris 1905; BT 404
151 Stelzer 1958, p. 21
152 Cf. Dieter Jähnig: Welt-Geschichte: Kunst-Geschichte. Zum Verhältnis von Vergangenheitserkenntnis und Veränderung. Cologne 1975, p. 197–218 (on Braque); cf. also Michael Bockmühl. Die Wirklichkeit des Bildes. Bildrezeption als Bildproduktion. Rothko, Newman, Rembrandt, Raphael. Stuttgart 1985; same author: Abstrakte Kunst und ästhetische Wirklichkeit. Zur Signatur der Moderne. In: "Info 3" magazine. 11.1987, p. 4–7
153 Otto Modersohn in: Ein Buch der Freundschaft. 1985, p. 16
154 26.11.1905; BT 425
155 8.11.1905; BT 424
156 To Marie Hill on 7.6.1905, BT 419; also 6.12.1905; BT 426
157 To Herma Becker on 1.12.1905; BT 425
158 5.11.1905; BT 420
159 11.12.1905; quoted after BT 427
160 20.12.1905; quoted after BT 428
161 Clara Rilke-Westhoff in: Ein Buch der Freundschaft. 1985, p. 46
162 16.1.1906; R.M. Rilke: letters 1902–1906. Leipzig 1930, p. 291
163 O. Reylaender-Böhme in: Ein Buch der Freundschaft. 1985, p. 40 and 41
164 A notable parallel to this, with the ideas consistently followed up, is found in: Henry Miller: The Colossus of Maroussi. 1940 quoted in the German paperback edition of 1965 (1985), p. 185 et seq. "The

essay on Balzac [. . .] only lent force to the idea that was beginning to crystallize within me: the idea that the artist's life, his dedication to art, is the highest and final phase of man's egocentricity. [. . .] To have a creative existence means – this is what I have found out – that one must become more and more selfless and live more and more in the world, identify oneself with it more and more, and thus influence it to the very marrow, so to speak. Like religion, art seems to me to be only a preparation, an introduction to true life. [. . .] To continue writing after one has reached the stage of self-knowledge seems to be fruitless and useless. The mastery of all forms of expression should definitely result in the final utterance – in the mastery of existence."

165 Summary of the most recent interpretations in Götte in Neuss catalogue, 1985, note 38

166 Busch 1981, p. 178

167 Götte, in Neuss catalogue, 1985, note 17

168 Krininger, 1986, p. 133

169 Murken-Altrogge, 1980, p. 114; cf. also p. 56

170 On this idea, mention may be made of observations by C.G. Jung (in: Psychologie und Dichtung [1930]. Collected Works, vol. XV. (4) 1984, p. 118). Although the text deals with poetry, it can be applied to any creative work. "Whether the poet knows that his work has been generated within him and is growing and maturing within him, or whether he imagines that he is creating his own invention by his own will – this does not alter the fact that his work is in reality growing out of him. It is like a child's relationship with its mother. The psychology of creativity is really a female psychology, because creative work grows from unconscious depths, from the mothers' realm as a matter of fact."

171 Cf. Aniela Jaffé: Bildende Kunst als Symbol. In: C.G. Jung and others: Der Mensch und seine Symbole. Olten and Freiburg im Breisgau 1968. 6th impression of the special 1982 edition, p. 240

172 24.2.1906; BT 434

173 Cf. Kirsch, 1987, p. 131

174 Fischerhude, Otto-Modersohn-Museum

175 2.3.1906; BT 436 Another source of information is a letter which Clara Rilke-Westhoff wrote to her husband on 8.2.1906 (printed in Renate Berger: Malerinnen auf dem Weg ins 20. Jahrhundert. Kunstgeschichte als Sozialgeschichte. Cologne 1982, p. 318 f., note 501). It gives an astonishing insight into Paula's many-sided psychology. Apart from her longing for more world and more art, it was her childlessness which had been oppressing her for years and was now among the reasons causing her to press for a separation. To be a proper woman, it was necessary for her to have had a child. "She herself believes in her ability to bear children, and would like to bear them at a later date when she herself is alone and dependent solely on herself, without a man being there," the letter states – a bewildering idea in those days, and still unconventional today. "It is very strange," Clara Rilke continues, "she still intends to do all this, and she wanted to explain to him that the last idea was her actual reason for leaving him. Because he does not understand the other reasons."

176 The statements which C.G. Jung, in several places, makes on the power of creativity are borne out by Paula's life and work, particularly in this phase. They also name the place from which such decisions can perhaps be most appropriately assessed: "The unborn work in the artist's soul is a natural force which prevails either by tyrannical power or by the subtle cunning of natural purposefulness, unconcerned with the personal well- being or grief of the person who is the vehicle of the creative power." (C.G. Jung: Über die Beziehungen der analytischen Psychologie zum dichterischen Kunstwerk [1922]. In: Collected Works, vol. XV. (4) 1984, p. 86)

177 8.5.1906; BT 445 f.

178 10.5.1906; BT 447

179 6.5.1906; quoted after BT 444

180 Was it consideration for the grief of the abandoned husband, was it opportunism, or was it his real opinion, when Bernard Hoetger wrote to Otto Modersohn in August 1906: "After all, we can only regard your wife's great talent as an uncultivated dowry which can blossom forth only if serious spiritual conflicts show that the gift of the dowry has after all been well cultivated and quiet thought induces her to make use of her talent." (Quoted after Kirsch 1987, p. 151) After Paula's death, Hoetger evidently continually asserted certain "discoverer's rights" or "rights of inheritance" in Paula Modersohn-Becker's works. The "displeasing mixture of reverence for the dead, art, and business sense" increasingly enraged Otto Modersohn. See on this subject Kirsch 1987, p. 143 f.

181 Letter to Otto Modersohn dated 15.5.1906; BT 448

182 To Otto Modersohn, 19.3.1906; BT 438 f.

183 Cf. in the following also Heinrich Wigand Petzet: Das Bildnis des Dichters, Paula Modersohn-Becker und Rainer Maria Rilke. Eine Begegnung. Frankfurt 1957

184 Petzet, 1957, p. 145 f., and after him G. Busch 1981, p. 60 f. and 160, also referred to the mask-like features of the Rilke portrait.

185 Cf. Karl Kerényi: Mensch und Maske. 1948. In: Eranos Jahrbuch 1948. Zurich 1949, p. 183–208; reprinted in: K. Kerényi: Humanistische Seelenforschung. Darmstadt 1966, p. 340–356. The Rilke portrait bears a striking resemblance to a classical Dionysus mask, which was formerly in the "Altes Museum von Berlin".

186 Diary, 3.9.1900; BT 233

187 17.10.1907; BT 475

188 Richard Pettit: Rainer Maria Rilke in und nach Worpswede. Lilienthal 1983, p. 215

189 Cf. v. Reinken 1983, p. 127

190 Cf. Hamburg catalogue 1976, p. 107

191 For example Margret Steenfatt: Ich, Paula. Die Lebensgeschichte der Paula Modersohn-Becker, Weinheim/Basle 1983. This book seems to be largely characterized by the authoress's own endeavours in the field of women's liberation, so that it contributes little to an adequate understanding of the artist and her work. It gives only summary regard to Paula's actual work.

192 See the letter from Otto Modersohn to Gustav Pauli dated 19.6.1919, printed in Murken-Altrogge, 1980, p. 117

193 According to statements made by Christian Modersohn, Fischerhude, November 1987

194 BT 463 f.

195 1987, p. 136

196 Bremer Nachrichten, issue of 11.11.1906; quoted after BT 463

197 18.11.1906; BT 464

198 Cf. C.G. Jung: Über die Beziehungen der analytischen Psychologie zum dichterischen Kunstwerk (1922). Collected Works, vol. XV. (4) 1984, p. 95

199 Otto Modersohn to Pauli, 19.6.1919, printed in Murken-Altrogge, 1980, p. 117

200 10.5.1907; BT 471

201 Cf. Busch 1981, p. 80, and Fritz Schmalenbach: Paula Modersohns Selbstbildnis mit dem Kamilienzweig. In: Neue Zürcher Zeitung, 15 Jan. 1961; reprinted in F. Schmalenbach: Studien über Malerei und Malereigeschichte. Berlin 1972, p. 88–89

202 Letter to her mother, 16.2.1907; BT 466

203 On colour symbolism in general, cf. Jolande Jacobi: Vom Bilderreich der Seele. Wege und Umwege zu sich selbst. Olten and Freiburg im Breisgau 1969. Special edition of 1981, esp. p. 88 and 140.
The last-mentioned interpretation was derived by Elisabeth Kübler-Ross and Gregg M. Furth from spontaneous drawings made by dying and seriously ill people. Cf. Gregg M. Furth: Die Verwendung von Zeichnungen, angefertigt in einer Lebenskrise. In: Elisabeth Kübler-Ross: Verstehen was Sterbende sagen wollen. Einführung in ihre symbolische Sprache. German edition Stuttgart 1982, p. 83–119

204 Cf. also Murken-Altrogge, 1980, p. 115

205 Cf. also Busch in Bremen catalogue 1976, No. 199

206 In the Eleusinian mysteries, poppy was offered up to Demeter as a symbol of the earth, and also of sleep and oblivion.

207 BT 473: The lines on Impressionism, quoted above, then follow in the letter: "I wanted to defeat Impressionism by trying to forget it. In this way I myself was defeated. We must work with the Impressionism which we have come to terms with and digested."

208 v. Reinken, 1983, p. 138

209 Cf. v. Reinken, 1983, p. 136

Index of Persons

Figures in *italics* refer to illustrations

Acknowledgement of illustrations

Jörg P. Anders, Berlin 79
Artothek, photograph by Joachim Bleuel, Planegg 28
Bremen Kunsthalle 26
The Detroit Institute of Arts 93
DuMont publishers, Cologne 51
Galerie Valentin, Stuttgart 49
Hamburg Kunsthalle (Elke Walford) 63, 109
Ralph Kleinhempel, Hamburg 56
Lars Lohrisch, Bremen 76, 78, 80, 91, 96
Museum Folkwang, Essen 94
Otto Modersohn-Museum, Fischerhude 29, 50, 61
Paula Modersohn-Becker Foundation, Bremen 14, 15, 18, 19, 27, 31, 34, 35, 36, 37, 46, 52, 55, 60, 62, 68 links, 69 unten, 70 links, 74, 77, 84, 85, 95, 98, 106, 107, 115
Picture archive of Preussischer Kulturbesitz Berlin 26
St. Etienne Gallery, New York 73
State Museum of Lower Saxony, Hanover, 30, 54 dust jacket motif
Von der Heydt Museum, Wuppertal 32, 90
Westphalian State Museum of Art and Cultural History, Münster 53, 89